How to crochet

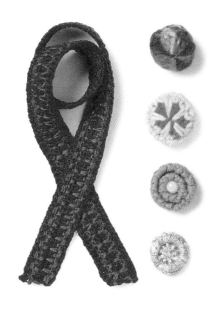

How to
crochet

The definitive crochet course, complete with step-by-step techniques, stitch libraries, and projects for your home and family

Pauline Turner

COLLINS & BROWN

To Kathleen, Rita, Sylvia, and all my students worldwide, both past and present—without whom this book would never have been written.

First published in Great Britain in 2001 by
Collins & Brown Limited
London House
Great Eastern Wharf
Parkgate Road
London SW11 4NQ

Distributed in the United States and Canada by
Sterling Publishing Co., 387 Park Avenue South, New York, NY 10016, USA

1 3 5 7 9 8 6 4 2

British Library Cataloguing-in-Publication Data:
A catalogue record for this book is available from the British Library.

ISBN 1 85585 827 4 (hardback edition)
ISBN 1 85585 942 4 (paperback edition)

Senior Editor: Clare Churly
Editor: Alison Leach
Consultant: Julia Barnard
Designer: Maggie Aldred
Photography: Nick Pope and Matthew Ward
Illustrator: Kuo Kang Chen

Reproduction by CK Digital, London
Printed and bound in the USA

This book was typeset using Bembo.

Contents

Introduction

CROCHET IS THE SIMPLEST CRAFT and also the most exciting. Don't believe me? At first I too had doubts; I thought that crochet was old-fashioned, with only old designs available, worked in colorless cotton. I began to learn the craft only because I had been ordered to teach it—and I was not at all happy.

Once I started to learn, I found that crochet is what you make it. I discovered that it was the youngest of all textiles; and of all the needlecraft and handicraft subjects I had taught, it was the only one that was not mechanized and had a freedom that was limitless. There are no rules in crochet, only guidelines. Indeed, the aim of this book is to encourage you to experiment, even if you are only a beginner. Every stitch in this book is explained. There are only three basic stitches—all other stitches are variations. You can use different-sized hooks to create different effects; and as for which yarn to use, you can use almost everything, as long as it is pliable—from wool to cotton thread, wire to string, strips of fabric to tissue paper. By the time you have finished this book, I hope that you will have the confidence to follow your own designs without reference to any pattern.

Crochet is for absolutely anyone with the will to pick up a crochet hook. May I wish you hours of happy crocheting.

CHAPTER ONE

Beginner's Workshop

CROCHET HAS NO RIGID RULES, only guidelines. There are good ways to work crochet and bad ways. The object of this book is to provide you with good ways which you can use as a guideline at all times to give that professional result. Crochet is the youngest of all fabric-making crafts. It began by imitating lace making, but the freedom of the crochet hook allows us to be imaginative, exploring color and texture, as well as producing the traditional fine-cotton openwork. Once the fabric has been produced, it can be used in whatever way you want, making items for the home, clothing, soft toys, and accessories.

Crochet is for everyone. The logically minded beginner may like to make notes and refer to these as their knowledge and skill increase, while the uninhibited, "let-it-happen" kind of person may wish to keep all their trial pieces and adventurously connect them into a throw or link them together to give an artistic 3-D display. For crochet to be rewarding and fun, you should choose whichever way of working you like best.

Hooks And Other Basic Equipment

Crochet is a portable craft requiring only a hook and yarn, some small sharp scissors, a measure (ideally with both inches and centimeters), and a large tapestry needle.

Right *So-called "regular" hooks are used with yarns and come in a variety of materials, most commonly plastic or aluminum. They are sized according to two parallel systems, from B to K and equivalent sizes 1 to 10½, ranging from smallest to largest. The numbers correspond to American knitting needle sizes. Long wooden hooks called "jumbo" (sizes 10, 11, 13, 15, and 16) are used for heavier items, such as rugs—as are plastic "jiffy" hooks (sizes Q and S). Most crochet hooks have a finger fold (flattened area) which helps to ensure a smooth working tension.*

Left *An afghan hook (far left) is necessary if you want to make Tunisian crochet (see pages 82–97), and you will need a jiffy lace needle (left) to work broomstick crochet fabric (see pages 130–139).*

Right *Fine steel hooks are for use mainly with cotton threads. They are sized by number, from 00 to 14; the larger the number, in this case, the smaller the hook. Steel hooks with thicker plastic handles are more comfortable to hold, especially for those with arthritic joints.*

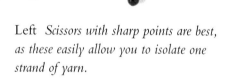

Left *Scissors with sharp points are best, as these easily allow you to isolate one strand of yarn.*

Right *A pliable tape measure with both standard and metric measures is best.*

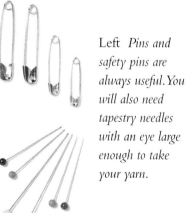

Left *Pins and safety pins are always useful. You will also need tapestry needles with an eye large enough to take your yarn.*

Hook Sizes

If you are working from an American pattern, the U.S. hook size will be specified (although you may need to change to a larger or smaller one to obtain the correct gauge). A British pattern will normally specify a metrically sized hook in the International Standard Range; see the chart opposite. You can buy these hooks in the United States (see pages 155–156); but you can use the equivalent American size instead, although these are not precise equivalents. Some American hooks give the size in millimeters along with the American size, but these sizes are not included in the International Standard Range. (You are unlikely to encounter patterns using the older British sizes of hook.)

Hook Size Conversion Chart

International Standard Range (ISR)	United States			Britain	
	Regular	Steel		Wool	Cotton [pre-metrification nos.]
10.00mm					
9.00mm	15 13			000 00	
8.00mm	12 11			0 1	
7.00mm	10½ 10	K J		2 3	
6.00mm	9	I		4	
5.50mm	8	H		5	
5.00mm	7			6	
4.50mm	6	G		7	
4.00mm	5	F		8	
3.50mm	4 3	E D		9	
3.00mm	2	C	0	10 11	3/0 2/0
2.50mm	1	B	1 2 3	12 13	0 1
2.00mm			4 5	14	1½ 2
1.75mm			6		2½ 3
1.50mm			7 8		3½ 4
1.25mm			9 10		4½ 5
1.00mm			11 12		5½ 6
0.75mm			13		6½
0.60mm			14		7 7½ 8

11

Yarns And Threads

Crochet is a bit of a pirate, stealing yarns, hooks, and even patterns from other crafts.
It can make use of almost anything that will bend and that is long enough—including wire, string,
strips of fabric, even tissue paper. But most crochet is worked in threads and yarns designed for this
craft—or for knitting—and they include a vast range of styles, thicknesses, and colors.

Left *The traditional thread for crochet is cotton, the most commonly used sizes ranging from 10 to 70; the larger the size number, the finer the thread. Cotton thread is normally mercerized to strengthen it and is recommended for heirloom work. All knitting yarns, whatever the fiber, can be crocheted.*

Above *Whether pure wool or a mixture of wool and manufactured fiber, fisherman yarn has a crispness that enables it to hold its shape and show the stitch definition to advantage. I recommend that you use this yarn when attempting a new process for the first time.*

Above *Silky yarns tend to slip and do not easily hold their form. In addition, the ends of the yarn have a tendency to come undone unless they have been very well secured.*

Right *Hairy yarns can hide the stitch structure and are difficult to pull back because the hairs lock into each other. This can be discouraging if you are learning a new process, so avoid hairy yarns until you are familiar with the stitch structure required. Fibers may also be lost if there is too much pulling back. Remember to face the light when working with very textured yarns. If the light is in front of you, it will shine through the holes, showing clearly where to insert the hook.*

Left *Fine yarns are not the best ones to choose to practice a new stitch construction if you have failing eyesight or if you suffer from stiff fingers. The use of a hook with a plastic handle can help with the gauge (see page 14), particularly if you are trying fine yarns for the first time.*

Below *Textured yarns, such as slubbed, bouclé, chenille, mohair, and brushed acrylics create an irregular gauge in the fabric, which is usually included as part of the design feature of the item being made. If you are a beginner, however, trying to get to know the different ways of making crochet fabrics accurately, you should leave the very textured yarns until you are sure of how the crochet fabric is being produced in the first place.*

Above *Nylon and many other synthetic fiber yarns have a tendency to stretch. Until you are confident in the way you hold the yarn, so that it flows freely through the fingers, there is a possibility that the gauge may go wrong: the yarn stretches and then, after the stitch has been made, it will relax, causing the stitch to be shorter than you expected and creating holes where the yarn should be acting as a filler.*

TIP

Dark colors can be difficult to see in dim or artificial lighting. This can cause eyestrain over a long period of time, so choose a project with light colors for dull days and evenings, reserving the darker ones for bright days. Remember too that crochet can make use of all types of unusual fabrics and be combined with just about every other type of craft. Don't restrict yourself, but experiment with everything in sight.

Measuring Gauge

Before you begin any project, take the time to crochet a gauge swatch. Gauge is an important part of any pattern, but is often ignored. It will determine the finished measurements of the piece, so you must have the same number of stitches and rows per inch (or centimeter) as the designer did. Even a small difference in gauge will alter the size of the design.

To make a gauge swatch, use the same hook, yarn, and stitch pattern as those to be used for the main work, and crochet a sample large enough to incorporate the pattern with at least 2in. (5cm.) additional width and length. Smooth out the sample on a flat surface. A flat surface is necessary if you are to get the gauge correct; using your knee, hand, or a chair arm may be convenient, but it will cause problems later. That extra tiny effort to get the gauge right really is worth it.

Smooth out the sample, but do not stretch it. Do not smooth the stitches from side to side—if you do that before measuring the sample, the finished project will end up too long and narrow. Make sure you smooth the sample from the base of the stitches to the top. The only exception to this rule is when the crochet is worked from side to side, so that the stitches lie horizontally.

Measure at least ¾in. (2cm.) in from the sides and at least 1¼in. (3cm.) up from the base; the first two to four rows tend to have a different gauge from the rest of the work. In addition, you should avoid including the last row worked in the measurement. What you are measuring is the number of stitches and also the number of rows. If you have too few of either—decrease the size of your hook. If you have too many—increase the size of your hook. The variation in gauge is caused by individual variations in *tension*—that is, the degree of tightness with which a crocheter works. (The word "tension" is also used in British patterns to denote gauge.) You may also find that your own tension varies wiht your state of mind while working; if you are feeling relaxed, the work comes out larger than if you are under stress. For this reason it is a good idea to re-check your tension occasionally.

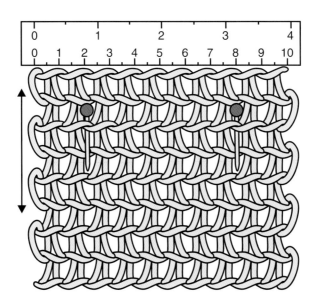

Place straight pins in the spaces between stitches for accurate counting.

Working From A Pattern

The pattern will tell you which yarn to use, the hook size, the gauge, and the size of the finished article. Patterns may be given in words or in symbols. A written pattern will list all abbreviations used. If the pattern is written in symbols, there will be a key to the symbols, either at the side of the stitch abbreviations or somewhere else in the pattern/book. Basic Information (see pages 149–156) has a comprehensive list of abbreviations and the respective symbol, if appropriate.

Points To Note When Reading A Written Pattern

• A crochet pattern will tell you where to put the number and type of stitches required for each step. This information is given in phrases or abbreviations between commas, or other punctuation marks. So read everything between the punctuation before executing the next step.

• If a pattern states "right side" after a row number, mark it with, for example, a loop of contrasting yarn. The basic crochet fabric stitches are identical on both sides, but some textured stitches (such as popcorns) and some multicolor patterns do have a right and wrong side. The distinction is also required in shaping a garment, as for the armholes.

• You normally insert the hook under the two strands of yarn that form the chain at the top of the loop, unless the pattern states otherwise. If you pick up the front or the back strand of yarn, the fabric will look different. When the pattern states "in chain space," you should insert the hook in the space beneath the chains and not in the stitches themselves.

• Different pattern producers and designers give different names to rows. The "Foundation Row" is the row worked into the chain, but in fact is rarely different from any other row. Therefore, a pattern may refer simply to "Row 1" or "First Row," rather than to a "Foundation Row."

• A pattern repeat within a row can be written in two ways. The most usual is by an asterisk. For example: ★2dc, ch2, skip 2sts, rep from ★ to last 2 sts.

This means that when the row is finished, there should be enough stitches for the repeat with two left over. Pattern instructions may read like this: ★2dc, ch2, skip 2sts, rep from ★ 4 times. This means that it must be worked five times in total before the next instruction.

The other way of indicating stitch pattern repeats in a row is to write within parentheses: "(2dc, ch2, skip 2sts) 4 times," means exactly that— in contrast to the asterisked instruction above, which must be worked five times.

• Crochet stitches are different heights. At the beginning of a row, a number of chain stitches need to be worked to lift the hook to the height of the stitches of that particular row; this is known as a turning chain. This turning chain forms the first stitch of the row and should be counted as such. If the pattern has different types of stitches in rows, the number of turning chain stitches required will be different at the beginning of the rows. Ignoring the turning chain results in the edges becoming either open and loose or tightly gathered, so that the article does not hang straight.

• Occasionally a pattern will entail working a "lifting chain" and placing the first stitch in the same place as the lifting chain. The lifting chain is then ignored and not included as a stitch.

Points To Note When Reading A Pattern In Symbols

Flat and lacy fabric designs are easier to read if symbols are used.
• Each symbol represents a stitch.

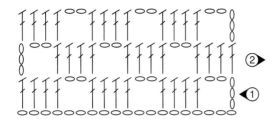

A stitch diagram with stitches being worked in rows

A stitch diagram with stitches being worked in a circle

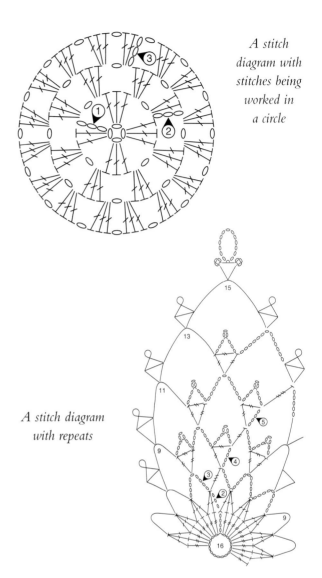

• Even if a pattern is written in symbols, the first two or three rows of the design will normally be written also in words. When worked in rows, the crochet is normally turned on each row. If a whole piece is worked in this way, the chains drawn at the start of a row indicate its beginning.

• Arrows will be shown at the side of a number or attached to a ring with a number inside. The number in the ring is the number of the row or round, and the arrow is the direction in which the row or round should be worked.

• Elaborately designed larger patterns for tablecloths or curtains will provide a detailed drawing of one of the designs in full, but will indicate the repeat with lines and number to show the number of turning chains required.

A stitch diagram with repeats

Getting Started

Ironically, it is the freedom of taking the hook in any direction, plus the numerous possible places in which to insert it into the fabric, that can be daunting. But you can master it.

For practice, a beginner should choose a regular hook (see page 10) that will not bend easily. Choose a medium-weight to heavy yarn, such as knitting worsted, with a size G/6 hook. A smooth yarn will make it easy for you to see the structure of the stitches—and to count them—and one made of wool has the advantage of being resilient (unlike cotton) and thus easier to control.

The structure of a crocheted stitch

The structure of a knitted stitch

Holding The Hook

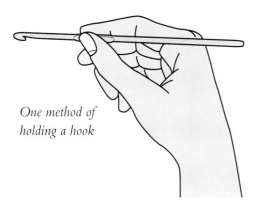

*One method of
holding a hook*

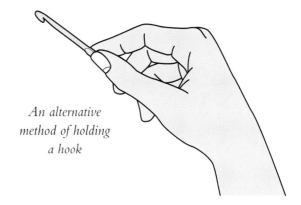

*An alternative
method of holding
a hook*

Try not to believe that there is only one way to hold the hook. If the way you hold your hook works—don't change it. The most important thing is not to grip the hook but to hold it gently and comfortably, as if you were writing with it. All diagrams show a right-handed worker. See Basic Information (pages 152–154) for left-handed diagrams. Hold the hook far down the stem, away from the head. The reason for this is that, to obtain the correct gauge, all loops placed around the crochet hook should fit the circumference of the stem exactly. The hook is narrower at the neck, and working in the neck of the hook will produce smaller stitches. Conversely, if the loops are larger than the stem and thus loose, it is equivalent to working with a larger hook.

Holding The Yarn

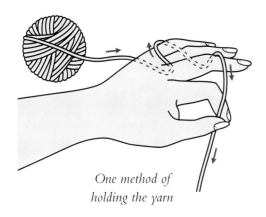

*One method of
holding the yarn*

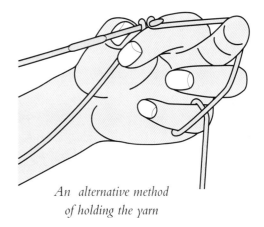

*An alternative method
of holding the yarn*

Hold the yarn round the little finger in a way that allows for a firm grip. This is appropriate for the finer cotton threads, but all other yarns have an elasticity which needs to be incorporated into the stitch as it is made. The yarn has to flow freely. If it pulls, it will become thinner; a yarn held too tightly may change from an worsted-weight thickness down to a sport-weight. Then once the yarn relaxes, holes will appear in the stitch. To avoid holding yarn too tightly, I suggest picking up the yarn between the middle and fourth finger. Drape it first over the fourth and little finger, then take it back under, allowing the yarn to come up and over the middle and index fingers. Hold the thread between the index finger and thumb. This leaves a space between the middle and index finger for the hook to be inserted to the left and under the yarn. Working instructions are "yarn over" (yo). If the hook snatches at the yarn from the top, the look of the stitch will vary from that of the pattern.

Slip Knot

All crochet fabrics begin with a single loop, or slip knot, on the crochet hook. This slip knot is there at the beginning and end of a stitch or fabric and is therefore never counted.

The following method of making a slip knot is most useful. The knot can be pulled up and closed, and so hidden in the fabric being made, rather than sticking out rather like a small pimple. The secret is to make sure the tail, or short end, is the one that tightens on the hook.

To make a slip knot, cross the tail end of the yarn over the main length of yarn coming from the ball, and form a loop. Then take this end over and behind the loop just made. Insert the hook under the single thread that has materialized as shown in diagram 10, going over both sides of the loop. Now tighten the slip knot on the hook by holding the thread from

the ball and the short end together, and pull the hook upward. At this stage the loop rarely fits snugly on the hook, but by pulling on the short end, you can make the correct size.

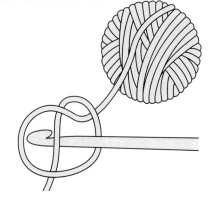

Making a slip knot

Chain (ch)

Chains are used as a base from which stitch patterns are made. They are also used to create holes in open and lacy patterns and for lifting the hook to the required height at the start of a new row or round.

Begin with a slip knot. Place the yarn over the hook from back to front as shown below and pull through the loop already on the hook—1ch made. Continue this process until you have the required length. Look at the chain and see how one side looks like embroidered chain stitch and the other

side is rough. Unless informed differently, always work with the smooth side facing you. Chains are used as a base from which stitch patterns are made. They are also used to create holes in open and lacy stitch patterns and for lifting the hook to the required height at the start of a new row or round.

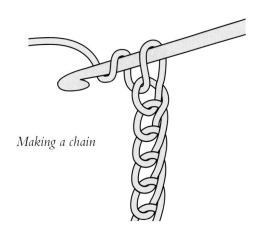

Making a chain

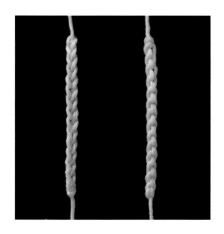

Here are two views of a crocheted chain— right side (left) and wrong side (right).

Slip Stitch (sl st)

A slip stitch is simply a chain that has been connected to the work. It can be used to carry a thread over a few stitches, which saves breaking off the yarn and starting again, or it can be worked to make chain-loop buttonholes.

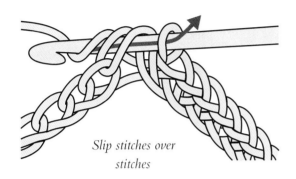

Slip stitches over stitches

Slip stitches as a join

Insert the hook into the stitch, put the yarn over the hook as for a chain (yo), picking up two strands as usual. Draw the thread through all the loops on the hook—sl st made. Slip stitches are normally used to link a stitch or group of stitches to another point. If you are using slip stitches to crochet a fabric, then pick up only the back strand; otherwise the fabric does not grow in height.

Fastening Off

After the final stitch has been worked, cut the yarn from the main ball leaving approximately 6 in. (15 cm.) Work ch 1 with this piece of yarn, but continue to pull it straight through the loop so that a little knot is formed. Slide the finger and thumb down this thread so that the knot tightens close to the work. If you wish to use the end of the yarn to join two pieces of work together, leave a longer end.

Slip stitches are commonly used when working flat motifs or tubes to join the rows into rounds.

Another useful characteristic of the slip stitch is its lack of height. It requires no turning chain at any time and therefore can be used to carry a yarn over stitches without having to break off and begin again. This means that there are two ends of yarn less to sew in!

Picot

A picot is made when a few chains are connected by a slip stitch producing a tiny loop, which stands up for a decorative effect. A picot is a traditional feature of the background net in Irish crochet—an example can be found in the stitch library on page 21. It can also form an attractive edge when used as the last row.

Chain And Slip-stitch Fabric

Even before you learn any other stitches, you can use the chain and slip stitch to make an open fabric to be used as a net. In fact, this fabric is the crochet version of the fisherman's net-making. Using twine, you can make a net for fishing or for the garden.

It is particularly difficult to measure the gauge of this fabric, simply because it stretches to any shape you wish—sideways, upward and diagonally. However, it does hang well and could therefore be used as the edging for a curtain. The elasticity in this fabric also makes it suitable for a foldaway shopping bag. Blankets created in this fabric trap the air to produce warmth without weight. Before starting on a larger project, work the following sample.

Practical Exercise: Network Pattern Of Slip Stitch And Chain

Work on a multiple of 4 chains plus 5 to get the correct size. Start with a small trial size.
Ch 29.
Row 1: sl st in 9th ch from hook ★ch5, skip 3ch, sl st in next ch, rep from ★ to end, ch6, turn— 6 loops made.
Row 2: ★sl st in 5ch sp, ch5, rep from ★ to last sp, sl st in 4th ch of last lp, ch6, turn.
Rep row 2 to desired length. If this is to be used as a gauge swatch, make sure you have worked enough rows.
The last row gives a scalloped edge. For a straight edge, work a final row working only ch2 instead of ch5.

Some Points To Note:

1 Once you have completed this gauge swatch, check that you have not made the chains too tight. If your fingers were hurting, then the chains are too tight!

2 When inserting your hook into the 5-chain space, remember that it goes under the chains and not into an individual chain stitch.

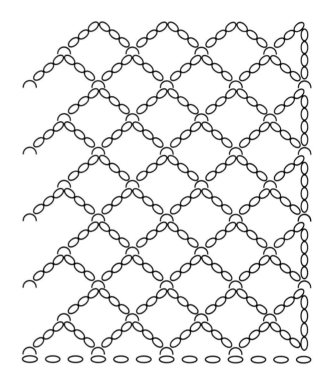

A stitch diagram of a network of chain and slip stitches

3 Counting the rows is easier if you count the diamonds and multiply the result by 2.

4 Drop the finished piece of crochet onto a smooth surface. Assuming that it has dropped flat, measure it where it lies without trying to smooth it out widthwise or lengthwise.

5 Because there is no right or wrong side to this reversible fabric, it will be easier to join two pieces together if you put the 6 ch sp loops together.

Stitch Library

Throughout this book you will find that the patterns in the stitch libraries use the skills you have learned in that particular workshop. Try working each of the patterns with different yarns and different hook sizes, and you will be amazed by how different the fabrics will look, even though you have used the same pattern. To help you make maximum use of the stitch libraries, make all the open patterns in thread and the rest in yarn. You could then join all the thread examples together to make a cloth, and all the yarn swatches together to make a lap rug.

In this beginner's workshop you have learned how to work chain stitch and slip stitch. The slip stitch can create both solid and lacy decorative fabrics. Try the two patterns below and see the difference.

Bosnian Stitch

You can produce a solid crochet fabric by just using chains and slip stitches. To work Bosnian stitch (also called English single crochet), you can start with any number of chains. Try a trial piece starting with 23 chains. Pick up the top strand of the chain for each st throughout.

Row 1: sl st in 3rd ch from hook, sl st in each ch to end, ch1, turn.

Row 2: ★1sl st in back loop of next st, rep from ★ to end, 1ch, turn. Rep row 2 to the desired length.

Picots

Picot fabric is traditionally used as a background for Irish crochet. Make a length of chain that can be divided by 4—each loop requires 4ch to start. Add 3 more chains to make the first loop to get around the corner to start the row off. Try beginning with 27 chains for a trial piece.

Row 1: sl st in 7th ch from hook. ★ch5, skip 3ch, sl st in next ch, ch3, sl st in same place [1picot made], rep from ★ to end.

Row 2: ch6, sl st in first ch sp, ★ch3, sl st in same place, ch5, sl st in next ch sp, from ★ to end. Rep row 2 to desired length.

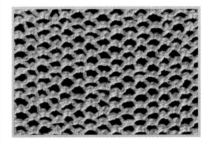

Project 1: Classic String Bag

This simple bag is crocheted with only the most basic of stitches—slip stitch and chain stitch—and the front and back are made together in a tube to avoid seams. The bag is worked with a fine yarn, but you may find it helpful to start with the simple alternative, using a heavier yarn and larger hook.

Materials

Size 20 tightly spun, mercerized crochet cotton, approx. 283yd. (260m.)
Size 4 steel (2.00mm) hook

Size

12 x 14in. (30 x 35cm.)

Gauge

10 loops should be close to 4in. (10cm.)

Notes

1 When making a tube, the work is not turned, and there is no real beginning or end after row 1.
2 *Optional.* If you leave a length of thread approximately 20in. (50cm.) long before making the slip knot, this length of yarn can then be used to sew up the base of the bag without joining in a new piece of cotton.
After working 10 to 20 lps of the second row or spiral, put a safety pin in the loop on your hook, to stop it from unraveling, and connect the chain into a circle. This will make it easier to know where to insert your hook when you come to the end of what is technically round 2.
You can be economical with your thread by working the handles first.

Handles

Make 6 lengths of chain each, 18in. (46cm.) long.

Bag

Ch244.
Row 1: sl st in 8th ch from hook, *ch5, skip 3ch, sl st in next ch, rep from * to end of ch (60 lps).
Rnd 2: Ch5, sl st in next ch sp (this is the space of the first lp made in row 1 and changes rows into rounds). *Ch5, sl st in next ch sp, rep from * in a continuous spiral until approximately 14in. (35cm.) in length has been completed, or until the thread runs out. Fasten off.

To Complete

Sew up the bottom of the bag by flattening the tube and joining the two halves of the tube together.
When the bag is flat there should be 30 loops on each side of the bag. Securely attach one end of a handle chain into the 5th, one into the 7th, and one into the 9th loop. Braid these three lengths of chain 2½in. (6cm.) from bag until 2½in. (6cm.) of chain are left. Securely join the three ends into the loops, skipping 12 loops free in the center.
Attach the remaining 3 lengths of chain to the other side of the bag in the same way.
Sew the braided strands togehter at each end of the plait to prevent unraveling.

> ### SIMPLE ALTERNATIVE
> *This bag is easily adapted using heavy cotton and a size F/5 (4.00mm) hook. Begin with 120ch, which will give you 30 loops at the end of row 1. When attaching the lengths of chain for the handles, place one chain in loop 2, one in 3, and one in 4, leaving 7 loops free in the center of each side.*

CHAPTER TWO

Stitch Workshop

THERE ARE THREE basic stitches in crochet: chain, single crochet, and double. Now you know the chain, have fun with the other two basic stitches. All other stitches are variations of these basic stitches. Where you insert your hook into the stitch, how many stitches are skipped, and how many stitches are worked into one place all change the look of the fabric you are making. Once you know the basic three stitch families, you can create all kinds of patterns by skipping stitches and replacing them with chains, putting several stitches into the same place, and even inserting the hook into a stitch in a different way. Many of these variations will be described in later workshops.

A slip stitch is a variation of a chain, but to make a solid fabric of just slip stitches can become tedious and rather slow, even though the finished effect is often worth the effort.

The crochet hook sits on top of the row being worked; therefore, turning chains to lift the hook need to be made at the start of each row. For each stitch described, the number of turning chains required will be given.

Single Crochet (sc) *(1 turning chain)*

First work a length of chain. Try 15 chains, so you have enough stitches to see how a piece of single crochet will look. The number of chains should equal the number of stitches required plus one—15 chains will make 14 stitches.

1 To work the first single crochet, first hold the smooth side of the chain facing you. Insert the hook into the third chain from the hook, front to back, under two strands of the chain. The two "skipped" chains equal the first stitch of the row—that is, one base chain, plus one chain for lifting the hook. Turning chains are counted as the first stitch unless the pattern tells you differently. Put the yarn over the hook (yo).

2 After you have put the yarn over the hook (yo), pull it through to the front.

3 There are now two loops on the hook; yo, pull through two loops—one single crochet made. Remember: all crochet stitches begin and end with one loop on the hook.

4 There are now two stitches completed (including the turning chain). The next single crochet is worked in the next chain, with no chains being skipped. Continue until all the chains are used. The number of stitches worked should then be one less than the number of chains you began with (include the turning chain as a stitch).

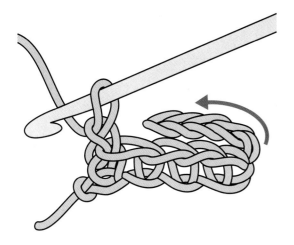

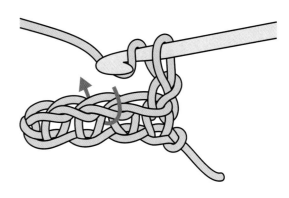

5 Second row: To help you to recognize the last stitch of a row and to keep sides straight , make 1 ch before turning the work. This means that the smooth side of the turning chain will be facing when the last stitch of the next row is made.

6 After turning the work, insert the hook into the next stitch. Remember that the first stitch is the turning chain, and therefore the first sc is technically worked in the second. Continue working 1sc in each st to the end of the row.

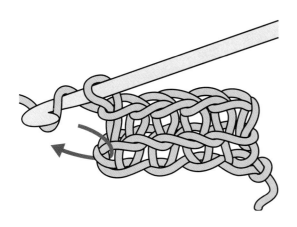

7 The very last stitch is worked in the turning chain. Repeat this row until the required length is reached.

Counting The Rows And Stitches

Looking at a piece of single crochet, you will see a strong, straight, horizontal line at regular intervals. Each line equals 2 rows. Between these lines is a row of horizontal dashes. Each dash is a stitch. Remember: the turning chain counts as one stitch, and you must include the very last "dash."

Single Crochet Rib

By reducing the hook size and altering where you put your hook in the stitch, you can create a ridged effect with an elasticized texture. Only a small number of stitches are required to make a waistband or cuff, and it is advisable to reduce the hook by one size for ribs on garments.

Where to insert the hook for a single crochet rib

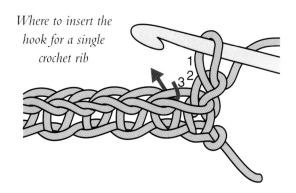

1sc in back loop of each st to end. The very last st is worked into the strand of yarn at the back of the "knot" made by the turning ch.

Work the first row into a starting chain exactly as usual.

Second row: ★1sc under back loop only of next st, rep from ★ to end, ch1, turn.

The crochet rib may produce irregular edges. This must be avoided if the rib is to be used for a waistband or cuff, simply because it is the side edge that becomes the finished edge of the garment. Turn the work toward you after working the ch1 to lift. Insert hook into back loop of third st down, counting the turning ch as the first st (see above).

TIP

If you are following a crochet pattern, it is a good idea to check where the pattern or book was published. The terminology in British crochet patterns differs significantly from that in American patterns: for example the U.S. "single" is called a "double" in Britain; the "double" is called a "treble," and so on. If you are in any doubt as to the pattern's origin, you will soon discover it when you measure your gauge swatch: if you get far fewer rows over the given measurement than specified, you are substituting taller American stitches for shorter British ones. A list of equivalent terms is given on page 151. You will find that once you get into the pattern, you can quickly translate the instructions mentally into American crochet terms.

Crab Stitch

There are many names for this stitch, including reverse single crochet, corded edge, rope stitch, Russian stitch, and shrimp stitch. It is really a single crochet worked backward.

Crab stitches are worked in the opposite direction from the rest of crochet—that is, from right to left instead of left to right (assuming that you are right-handed).

Work them on the right side of a fabric as an edging or finishing row, using a hook one size smaller than for the main fabric. The whipped look of this stitch is more pronounced if the right side is facing. You do not need to work a turning chain if you are working crab stitches in the round (rather than a row). However, for a crisp corner, work ch1 at a straight edge.

Insert the hook into the next stitch to the right, picking up two strands of yarn as for a normal single crochet. Collect the yarn by dropping the hook head onto the thread (see right). Bring the thread through to the front of the work, tilting the hook upward to make sure there are two loops on the hook. It is very easy at this stage to pull the yarn through the loops, which would turn the stitch into a backward slip stitch. Twist the hook to a normal working position, yo, then draw through the two loops—and one crab stitch is complete.

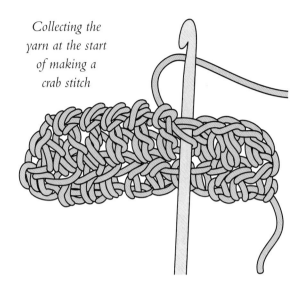

Collecting the yarn at the start of making a crab stitch

Double Crochet (dc) *(3 turning chain)*

If you loop the yarn over the hook before inserting it into the work, you will make a taller stitch than a single crochet. The yarn can be looped once, twice, or more times, as you will see on the following pages. One of the most commonly used of these taller stitches is double crochet, which is about twice the height of single crochet. To lift the hook to the correct height for double crochet, you need to work three turning chains.

1 Work a length of chain, but no more than 20. The number of chains should equal the required number of stitches, plus 2. Then put the yarn over the hook. Have the smooth side of the chain facing and insert the hook under 2 strands of the fourth chain; yo and pull through. There are now 3 loops on the hook.

2 Yo and pull through 2 loops to leave 2 loops on the hook, yo and pull through the remaining 2 loops so you are back to 1 loop on the hook—one double crochet made. Work a double in each stitch to the end, ch3, turn.

3 Now you are ready to start Row 2. With a double it is an easy mistake to put the first stitch in the same place as the 3ch. If you do this you will either increase by 1 st or produce a wavy edge which makes for difficult joining.

For a straight edge, work the first double (2nd st) into the stitch beside the turning chain. Continue placing 1dc in each stitch to the end, remembering to place a double in the top of the turning chain from the last row.

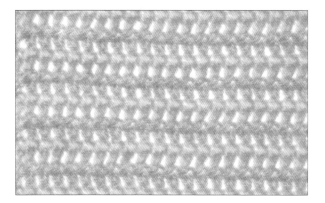

> ### TIP
> *If you work primarily with yarn rather than with thread, you may find that two turning chains are sufficient for a treble. If you find there is a hole at the start of the rows, reduce the number of chains by one. Working with finer threads and smaller hooks normally means using the traditional three chains.*

Other Basic Fabric Stitches

Taller stitches are made by wrapping the yarn one more time around the hook before placing the hook into the work. The taller the stitches are, the more open the fabric will be.

Stitch Heights

Early in the twentieth century, when cotton crochet was at its most popular, a row of single crochet was often worked into the foundation chain prior to introducing the pattern. Today this is not recommended, particularly when working a fabric incorporating taller stitches. Taller stitches are those stitches that have the yarn wrapped around the hook before it is inserted into another stitch. The short stitches (those without any yarn wrapped around the hook) will tighten the work widthwise. The more wraps placed around a hook, the taller the stitch will become. The taller the stitches become, the greater the spread. This means that beginning a work with a row of single crochet (a short stitch) will produce a "plant-pot" look in a fabric made of taller stitches.

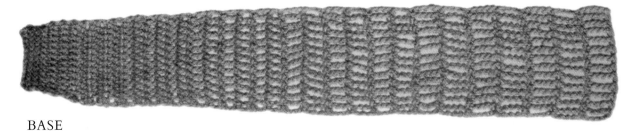

BASE

TOP

Triple Crochet (tr) *(4 turning chains)*

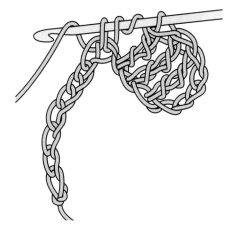

Wrap the yarn around the hook twice, then insert it into the 5th chain from the hook, yo and pull through to the front; with 4 loops on the hook. ★yo, pull through 2 loops, rep from ★ twice to leave one loop on the hook. Continuing making 1tr in each ch to end, ch4, turn.

Double Triple (dtr) *(5 turning chains)*

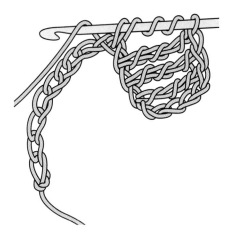

To make a double triple, wrap the yarn over the hook 3 times. Insert hook into the sixth chain from the hook, yo and pull through to the front to leave 5 loops on the hook. (Yo and pull through 2 loops) 4 times to leave one loop on the hook. Continue making 1dtr in each chain to end, ch5, turn.

Triple Triple (tr tr) *(6 turning chains)*

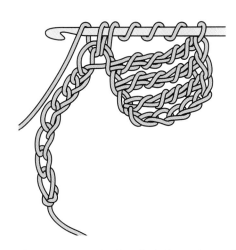

Wrap the yarn over the hook 4 times, insert hook into the 7th ch from the hook, yo and pull through to the front to leave 6 loops on the hook. (Yo and pull through 2 loops) 5 times. Continue making 1tr tr in each chain to end, ch6, turn.

Half Double (hdc) *(2 turning chains)*

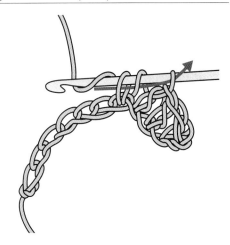

The height of the half double is somewhere between a single crochet and a double. When the stitch is completed, it does not look like an embroidered chain that uses two strands of yarn, but more like a double chain using three strands of yarn.

Wrap the yarn around the hook and insert it into the 4th chain from the hook exactly as if you were making a double. Yo and pull through to the front; with 3 loops on the hook. Yo and pull through all 3 loops at once to make the stitch shorter than a double.

31

Basic Edgings

*Edgings in crochet are easy and can be worked directly into woven or knitted fabric.
Besides being used on the edge of a piece of crochet fabric, they can be added at the same time
as two pieces are joined together to decoratively embellish the design.*

• One row of sc followed by one row of slip stitch with a picot in every third stitch takes away the straight edge to give an interesting finish.

• Crab stitch worked over one row of single crochet takes away the chain look of a crochet stitch and gives a firm, attractive edge.

• A shell edge is another popular finish for a knitted or crocheted article.

To make a shell edge, check that stitches can be divided by 6 with 1 left over.

With RS facing join in yarn, ★skip 2sts, 5dc in next st, skip 2sts, sl st in next st, rep from ★ to end. Fasten off.

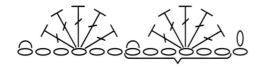

A stitch diagram of a shell edge. The bracketed section of the diagram shows one repeat of six stitches.

TIP

It is not always easy to keep an even gauge with very long stitches; they have a habit of breaking away from their neighbors. When you wrap the yarn around the hook, keep your finger on each wrap made so that it remains the size of the circumference of the hook stem. Release your finger from these wraps only as you work them off the hook.

Adding an edging to your crochet can make all the difference to the final look of the item.

Stitch Library

Endless stitch patterns can be designed using the three basic stitches. Try the examples in this stitch library to get yourself started.

"V" Stitch

Work an even number of chains, for example 24.

Row 1: 2dc in 4th ch from hook, ★ skip 1ch, 2dc in next ch, rep from ★ to last 2sts, skip 1 st, 1dc in last st, ch2, turn.

Row 2: ★2dc in center of 2dc gr, rep from ★ to last st, 1dc in last st, ch2, turn.

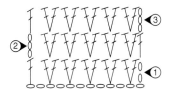

Open And Close

Ch32 (or a multiple of 10, plus 2).

Row 1: 1dc in 4th ch from the hook, ★skip 1ch, (4dc, ch2, 1dc) in next ch, skip 3ch, 5dc, rep from ★ to last 7ch, skip 1ch, (4dc, ch2, 1dc) in next ch, skip 3ch, 2dc, ch3, turn.

Row 2: 1dc in next dc, ★(4dc, ch2, 1dc) in 2ch sp, 5dc, rep from ★ to end finishing with 2dc

instead of 5dc, ch3, turn.
Rep row 2 to desired length.

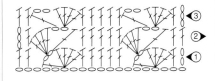

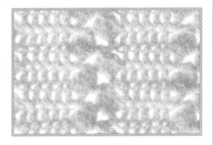

Crazy Stitch

Work an even number of chains, for example 24.

Row 1: 1sc in 4th ch from hook, ★1dc in next ch, 1sc in next ch, rep from ★ to end, ch3, turn.

Row 2: 1sc in next dc, ★1dc in next sc, 1sc in next dc, rep from ★ to end, ch3, turn.

Rep row 2 to desired length.

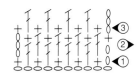

Shell Stitch

Make a chain that can be divided by 6 plus 1, for example 25ch.

Row 1: 5dc in 4th ch from hook, skip 2ch, 1sc in next ch, ★skip 2ch, 5dc in next ch, skip 2ch, 1sc in next ch, rep from ★ to end, ch3, turn.

Row 2: 2dc in same place as turning ch, skip 2sts, 1sc in next dc (central dc of 5dc gr), ★5dc in sc, 1sc in central dc of gr, rep from ★ to end, 3dc in turning ch. There are no turning chain for row 3.

Row 3: ★5dc in sc, 1sc in central dc of gr, rep from ★ to end, ch3, turn.

Rep rows 2 and 3 to desired length.

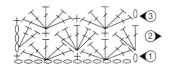

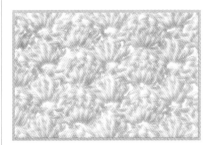

Staggered Single Crochet

Make an even number of chains.

Row 1: 1sc in 5th ch from hook, *ch1, skip 1ch, 1sc in next ch, rep from * to end, ch1, turn.

Row 2: 1sc in ch sp, *ch1, skip 1sc, 1sc in next ch sp, rep from * to last st, 1sc in turning ch, ch3, turn.

Row 3: Skip 1sc, 1sc in next ch sp, *ch1, skip 1sc, 1sc in next ch sp, rep from * to last st, 1sc in turning ch, ch1, turn.

Rep rows 2 and 3 to desired length. Make sure that you go into the space below the chain and not into the chain.

Counterpane Stitch

This is a variation of sc, but taller, being of a similar height to a half double. Work any number of chains, one for each of the stitches needed, plus 2; for example 24. Insert the hook into the stitch, yo, draw through to front, yo and pull through one loop only, yo and draw through both loops on hook—1 counterpane stitch made.

Row 1: Insert hook in 4th ch from hook, 1 counterpane st in each ch to end, ch2, turn.

Row 2: Insert hook in next st, 1 counterpane st in each st to end, ch2, turn.

Rep row 2 to desired length.

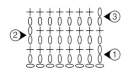

Alternate Sc And Dc

Make any number of chains. Ideally start and end this fabric with one row of sc.

Row 1: 1sc in 3rd ch from hook, 1sc in each ch to end, ch3, turn.

Row 2: 1dc in next st, 1dc in each st to end, ch1, turn.

Row 3: 1sc in next st, 1sc in each st to end, ch3, turn.

Rep rows 2 and 3 to desired length.

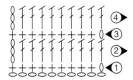

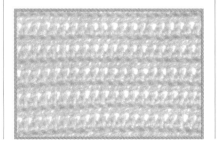

Peacock Eye

Ch26 (or a multiple of 8, plus 2 for turning).

Row 1: 9tr in 6th ch from hook, skip 3ch, 1sc in next ch, *skip 3ch, 9tr in next ch, skip 3ch, 1sc in next ch, rep from * to end.

Row 2: ch6, * 1sc in 5th tr of gr, ch2, (1tr, ch1, 1tr) in sc, ch2, rep to last group, 1sc in 5th tr of group, ch2, 1tr in turning ch, ch4, turn.

Row 3: 4tr in same place as turning ch, *1sc in sc, 9tr in 1ch sp, rep from * to last sc, 1sc in sc, 5 tr in last st, ch4, turn.

Row 4: *(1tr, ch1, 1tr) in sc, ch2, 1sc in 5th tr of gr, ch2, rep from * to last sc, (1tr, ch1, 1tr) in sc, ch2, 1sc in last st, ch1, turn.

Row 5: * 9tr in 1ch sp, 1sc in sc, rep from * to end.

Rep rows 2–5 until you have the desired length.

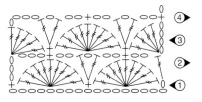

Project 2: Padded Coat Hangers

The beauty of these padded coat hangers is their simplicity, each one showcasing a different stitch. Alternatively, any of the coat hanger patterns can be worked as a rectangular piece of fabric and made into a pencil case or eyeglasses case, and a button loop and button can be added as a fastener.

Pink Coat Hanger

Materials

Sport-weight cotton yarn, approx. 75yd. (70m.) in pink
Size F/5 (4.50mm) hook
Wooden hanger 16in. (42cm.) wide
¼yd. (25cm.) quilter's batting for padding
½yd. (50cm.) narrow ribbon
For the decoration:
3 purchased roses or scraps of size 10 crochet cotton to make the crochet flowers and leaves (optional)
Size 6 steel (1.75mm) hook

Size

To fit a wooden hanger 16in. (42cm.) wide. However, the pattern can be adapted to fit any hanger.

Gauge

12sts to 3in. (7.5cm.), 4 rows to 2in. (5cm.)

To Make

Ch 69.
Row 1: 1hdc in 4th ch from hook, 1hdc in each ch to end, ch2, turn (67sts).
Row 2: 1hdc in each st to end, ch2, turn.
Rep row 2 10 times.
Work 1 row crab stitch. Fasten off.

To Complete

Pad the hanger with the batting. Fold the crochet over the hanger, making sure the crab-stitch edge is at what is to be the front of the hanger. Sew the cover in place, catching the foundation chain to the base of the crab-stitch edge. Leave 2 chains unattached at the base of the hook.

Rose Decoration

Ch49.
Row 1: 1sc in 4th ch from hook, ★ch2, skip 2ch, 1sc in next ch, rep from ★ to end, ch1, turn (16sps).
Row 2: 3sc in sp, (3sc in next sp) 3 times, (4dc in next sp) 3 times, (5dc in next sp) twice, 4tr in next sp, (5tr in next sp) twice, 4dtr in next sp, (5dtr in next sp) twice, 3dtr in last sp.
With RS facing, and starting at the beginning of row 2, roll up the work, and sew the roll together through the foundation chain to form a rose.

Leaf Decoration

Ch 11, 1sc in 2nd ch from hook, 1sc, 1hdc, 3dc, 1hdc, 2sc, 3sc in last ch, cont working down the other side of the foundation ch until you return to the slip knot with 2sc, 1hdc, 3dc, 1hdc, 1sc, 2sc in last ch, join with sl st. Fasten off.

Hook Cover

Join yarn to one of the unsewn foundation chains. Sl st around the hook to the tip. Fasten off.
Finally, tie the ribbon into a bow at the base of the hook, and attach the roses.

Blue Coat Hanger

Materials

Sport-weight cotton yarn, approx. 75yd. (70m.) in blue
Size E4 (3.50mm) hook
Wooden hanger 16in. (42cm.) wide
¼yd. (25cm.) quilter's batting for padding

Size

To fit a wooden hanger 16in. (42cm.) wide. However, these can be adapted to fit any hanger.

Gauge

10sts and 9 rows to 2in. (5cm.)

To Make

Ch82.
Row 1: 1sc in 3rd ch from hook, 1sc in each ch to end, ch1, turn (81sts).
Row 2: *1tr, 1sc, rep from * to end.
Row 3: 1sc in each st to end, ch1, turn.
Rep rows 2 and 3 nine more times.
Work 1 row crab stitch. Fasten off.

To Complete

Work as given for the Pink Coat Hanger.

Hook Cover

Work as for Pink Coat Hanger, excluding decorations.

Mauve Coat Hanger

Materials

Sport-weight cotton yarn, approx. 75yd. (70m.) in mauve
Size G6 (4.50mm) hook
Wooden hanger 16in. (42cm.) wide
¼yd. (25cm.) quilter's batting for padding

Size

To fit a wooden hanger 16in. (42cm.) wide. However, the pattern can be adapted to fit any hanger.

Gauge

2 shells to 3in. (7.5cm.); 3 rows to 2in. (5cm.)

To Make

Ch67.
Row 1: 5dc in 5th ch from hook, skip 2ch, 1sc in next ch *skip 2ch, 5dc in next ch, skip 2ch, 1sc in next ch, rep from * to end, ch3, turn.
Row 2: 2dc in same place as turning ch, *1sc in center dc of 5dc shell, 5dc in next sc, rep from * to last shell, 1sc in center dc, 3dc in last st of row (there is no turning chain).
Row 3: *5dc in next sc, 1sc in center dc of shell, rep from * to end placing the last sc on top of the turning ch, ch3, turn.
Rep row 2 once.
Fasten off. (One side of the cover is now complete.)
Rejoin yarn to foundation chain. Work row 2 into the foundation chain using the same chains as for the first side. Work row 3 once and rows 2 and 3 once again.

To Complete

Pad the hanger with the batting. Fold the crochet over the hanger so that the shell edges of row 5 make a pretty scalloped finish. Join the cover over the padding by sewing the two pieces together at the top, catching the shells in the double crochet stitches in a straight line with the sc.

Hook Cover

Join yarn to a stitch at the base of the coat hanger hook and sl st around the hook to the tip. Fasten off.

Project 3: Book Covers

These book covers are made in single crochet with a final round in crab stitch, and the larger book cover has a crochet panel applied with blanket stitch. If desired, a cross stitch pattern or name can be added to the panel using the single crochet squares for the cross stitch.

Materials

Size 20 tightly spun, mercerized crochet cotton, approx. 283yd. (260m.) in red or green
Approx. 142yd. (130m.) of the same in cream for the panel
Size B/1 (2.00mm) hook
1 button (see pages 145–6 for how to crochet buttons)
10in. (25cm.) lining material (optional)
Large book measuring 6½ x 9in. (16 x 23cm.)
Small book measuring 4½ x 7in. (11 x 17.5cm.)

Size

Large book cover 9 x 14in. (23 x 36cm.)
Large book panel 4¼ x 6in. (11 x 15cm.)
Small book cover 7¼ x 9¾in. (18 x 25cm.)

Gauge

6sts and 8 rows to ¾in. (2cm.)

To Make

For the large book cover work the number of stitches given in the brackets. The final round includes a buttonhole. If you prefer to sew a loop to the book cover after it has been completed, omit the buttonhole and proceed all the way around the cover with crab stitch (see pages 28–29).
Ch56(72).
Row 1: 1sc in 3rd ch from hook, 1sc in each ch to end, ch1, turn (55[71]sts).
Row 2: Ch1 (counts as first st), 1sc in next st, 1sc in each st to end, ch1, turn.
Rep row 2 until 138 rows have been completed, or until required length has been reached. Do not break off yarn. Continue working down the panel in sc as an edging placing 3sc over 4 rows. (If you place 1sc per row the border will not lie flat.) Put 1 extra sc in the corner and continue with 1sc in each foundation chain to next

corner. Put 1 extra sc in the corner and continue with sc placing 3sc over 4 rows. Put 1 extra sc in the corner, 25[33]sc, ch6, skip 5sc, 25[33]sc to complete all around the cover. Join with sl st.
Final round: Crab stitch in each st to 6ch, turn work and place 7sc in chain loop, turn work, and continue all around the book cover without any additional stitches until you reach the first crab stitch made. Fasten off.

Panel

It is most important to make sure that the sides are neat and the gauge is the same throughout.
Ch35.
Row 1: 1sc in 3rd ch from hook, 1sc in each chain to end, 1ch, turn (34sts).
Row 2: Ch1 (counts as first st), 1sc in next st, 1sc in each st to end, ch1, turn.
Rep row 2 until 56 rows have been completed, or until required length has been reached.

To Complete

Carefully measure the fabric of the cover of the book, and mark out the position of the panel. Using a contrasting but complementary thread, blanket-stitch the panel in place. Attach the button to correspond to the button loop.

SIMPLE ALTERNATIVE
Cover a book with fabric, by making and joining two pockets into which the book can be slipped. Make the panel in crochet as above. Attach the panel to the fabric cover with blanket stitch. Make a button loop. Sew the button to the cover to correspond to the position of the button loop.

CHAPTER THREE

Color
Workshop

INTERESTING TWO-COLORED AND MULTICOLORED EFFECTS can be achieved in crochet, often by very simple means. Some of these techniques involve using more than one color within a row, but others can be achieved using only one color at a time. With crochet, if you wish to introduce color, there is total free choice in how to use it. All things are possible in crochet with a little experimentation. For example, you can achieve interesting results by placing shorter stitches in the same row as longer stitches when working stripes. Or you can insert your hook into the base of a stitch, rather than the top, to produce blips of color that drop into the shade used on the previous row.

The fact that there is only one loop on the hook at any one time allows color to be introduced in quite a free way. In this workshop new colors will be introduced into a fabric using only one yarn per row or round.

Choosing The Color

Some people have a "flair" for color. Others think they have no "color sense." Indeed, I was thrown out of the art class in school and told I would never do anything creative—I believed it! I have since proved the teacher wrong. So if you think you are not "good with color," follow these simple steps and you will be amazed by what you can do.

• For your first project involving two or more colors, choose tones from the same segment of the color wheel. The result may be a little muted, but it will be pleasing to the eye; the yarns will work together even if you do not initially understand what is happening.

• For your second color project, be bold: select yarns from one segment of the color wheel, but also take a very bright color from the segment that is lying exactly opposite. Add a tiny touch of this color here and there, and you will see that it acts as an accent.

• Play with random color. Mix up small pieces of yarn. Close your eyes, knot two pieces together and begin winding the yarn into a ball. As you reach the end of each piece, knot another piece to it. The aim of this color exercise is to produce a randomly colored ball that will show you how colors work together—or don't!

• Take a smooth yarn to use as a base of double crochet fabric. On alternate rows, work one row single crochet using a space-dyed or multicolored yarn. This give the illusion of having used many different yarns.

• Make the examples in the stitch library, using firstly dark and light tones of the same color; secondly a dull color and a contrasting bright color; thirdly, use two bright, pure colors for the same stitch pattern. See which you prefer, and initially confine yourself to using these combinations when making a large project. It is worth remembering that most people will lean toward colors in only one half of the color spectrum. If someone does not like your choice of colors, they may not easily like any of your color combinations, preferring the other half of the color spectrum. (Of course, this works both ways, and you might not like their color choice!)

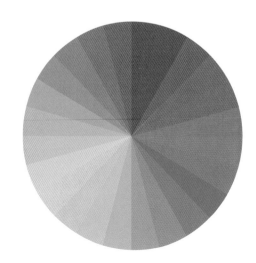

A color wheel provides a quick reference to remind you how different colors work together.

Camouflage

When working with colors, you may find that some combinations do not work. Don't be alarmed—there are three basic strategies to alter the overall look of the colors chosen.

• If you are not sure if the colors will marry before you start, take a complementary thread and work it together with the yarn. This will soften a harsh color. It is particularly helpful when using yarns that have different textures, thicknesses, and colors. You can crochet with many threads at once without previously twisting them together into one yarn. Using yarns of different thicknesses, as well as colors, is easy.

• Use an embroidery technique such as chain stitch or cross stitch to disguise a problem area, adding it to the project after the crochet has been worked.

• Simply over-dye the whole project. A light color bath will blend into all the colors in the project to give it an overall color with varied tones. This will dim the brighter colors but give a shadow throughout the article that is complementary and softening to any contrast you do not like.

Adding A New Color

When changing color—especially within a row—it is important to avoid a "color drag." This happens when the old color "seeps" into the first stitch worked in the new color and is caused by the way crochet stitches are formed, with interlocking loops. You can avoid this by following the steps given below.

The most important point to remember when adding a yarn of a different color is to add it before the last stitch is complete—that is, when there are still two loops left on the hook. If you complete the stitch and then add the new color, you will drag the old color into the new one because the first chain will be of the old color.

This way of introducing a new color is as important in the middle of a row as it is at the edges.

It is worth going to the trouble of working the trial piece in the practical exercise over the page and reading the explanatory notes given with each new process.

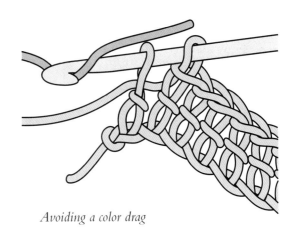

Avoiding a color drag

Practical Exercise: Color Works

Crochet does not have to turn on each row. To give you greater freedom when working different articles, complete this exercise piece and take note of all the professional ideas it shows you.

Use two colors of the same thickness, choosing either two contrasting colors (from opposite sides of the color wheel) or contrasting tones of the same color (one very dark and one very pale). Choose an appropriate hook for the thickness of yarn; for example, a worsted-weight yarn with a G/6 (4.50 mm) hook. The first color is abbreviated M for "main" and the second color C for "contrast." A point to remember with this piece of work is to count each row to make sure you have 15 stitches, as it is easy to lose a stitch whenever the work is not turned on each row. Because you do not turn your work on each row, you have to use a different hook-insertion technique on alternate rows. When crochet is not turned, the place to put the hook is to the right of the first stitch immediately below, and not to the left. You put your hook in the chain top at the left-hand side of a stitch only after the work has been turned.

Begin with 17 chains in M.

Row 1: 1dc in 4th ch from hook, dc to end (15 sts), join in C before last stitch is complete (see page 43) ch1, turn work.

Row 2: ★1tr, 1sc, rep from ★ to end. Place the last loop on a safety pin. Do not turn the work.

Row 3: Insert the hook into the first stitch (1ch) at the beginning of the row. With M ch3. 1dc in each st to last st, check that you have 14 sts before working the last st. Work the last dc by inserting the hook into the stitch as usual, but before collecting the yarn to bring through to the front, place the loop from the safety pin on your hook, yo, draw through the 3 strands of yarn to lock the st (2 from the top of the st and 1 from the safety pin), yo and pull through 2 loops (2 loops remain on hook). Change to C to complete the last st, ch1, turn.

Row 4: dc to end, leaving last st on a safety pin.

Row 5: as row 3.

Row 6: ★1tr placed in the bottom of the next dc, 1sc, rep from ★ to end placing loop in safety pin.

Rows 7–9 as rows 3–5.

Rows 2–9 form a repeat pattern. Work the repeats until you feel comfortable with the new techniques. If you wish to put the above pattern into an article, there is more color and stitch balance if you finish on row 5.

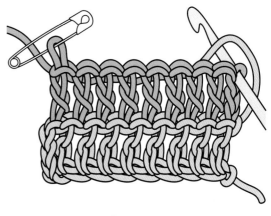

Diagram 1

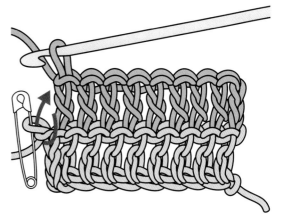

Diagram 2

Stitch Library

Experiment with the selection of stitch patterns given in this library, worked in a main color (M) and a contrasting color (C). Choose a design you like, and try it using different color combinations.

Bee Stitch

Bee stitch forms a textured stripe that avoids the ruler-like precision of most color stripes. Work a trial piece starting with the main color (M) and an odd number of chains.

Row 1: 1dc in 4th ch from hook, 1dc in each ch to end, change to contrast (C), turn work.

Row 2: No turning ch. *1dc, sl st, rep from * to end, do not turn work.

Row 3: In M ch3, dc to end, change to C, turn work.

Row 4: Ch1, sc to end.

Row 5: As row 3.

Rep rows 2 to 5 for the desired length.

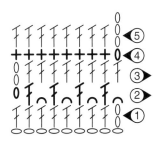

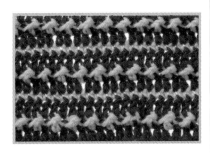

Vertical Stripes

This is one method of producing vertical stripes using two colors but still working from bottom to top. It uses only one color in each row, but the chains made in each row will be encased in the double crochet stitches of the next row. There is no need to break off the yarn; simply turn on every two rows. Try a piece using 29ch in the main color.

Row 1: 1dc in 4th ch from hook, 1dc, *ch3, skip 3ch, 3dc, rep from * to end, change to C color in last st, turn.

Row 2: *Ch3, skip 3 sts, 3dc worked over the chain and into the 3 skipped sts, rep from * to last 3sts, ch2, skip 2 sts, sl st in top of turning ch with M, turn.

Row 3: Ch3, 2dc, *ch3, skip 3ch, 3dc, rep from * to end changing color in last st, turn.

Rows 2 and 3 form the pattern. Rep to desired length.

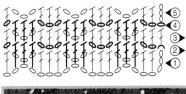

Seed Stitch

Seed stitch is ideal for varying the amount of color you need in a crochet fabric. The number of stitches required is a multiple of 3, plus turning ch. Make a trial piece with 24ch, starting with the main color.

Row 1: 1dc in 4th ch from hook, 1dc, *ch1 (do not skip a ch) 3dc, rep from * to end. Join in C. No turning chain needed; turn work.

Row 2: Ch2, *1sc in 1ch sp, ch2, rep from * to end, 1sc in last st. Do not turn work.

Row 3: Sl st into 2ch sp, ch2, 2dc in same space, *ch1, 3dc in 2ch sp, rep from * to end. Join in C, turn work.

Rep rows 2 and 3 to the desired length.

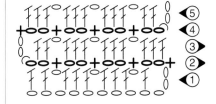

Crosshatch Stitch

Double crochet stitches change direction, giving the stripes a chevron look. This piece begins with 28ch in main color (M).

Row 1: 2dc in 4th ch from hook, *skip 3ch, 1sc in next ch, ch3, 3dc (using foundation chain), rep from * to last 4ch, skip 3ch, 1sc in last ch.

Row 2: Ch3, 2dc in sc, * skip 3dc, 1sc in first of 3ch, 2dc, 1dc in sc, rep from * to last 3sts, skip 2dc, 1sc in top of turning ch changing to C.

Rep row 2 as a pattern to desired length, changing colors in the last st of every other row.

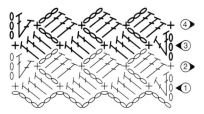

Box Stitch

Lond quadruple triples, formed by wrapping the yarn 5 times around the hook, form the verticles in this 2-color pattern. The trail piece begins with 27ch in C.

Row 1: 1dc in 4th ch from hook, dc to end, change to M, ch3, turn.

Row 2: dc to end, ch3, turn.

Row 3: dc to end, change to C looping the yarn through the back side of the M sts of rows 2 and 3, ch3, turn.

Row 4: 1dc, * 1 quadruple tr hooked into the front of the second st of the previous C row, 3dc, rep from * to last 3 sts, 1 quadruple tr hooked into previous C row, 2 dc. Leave loop on safety pin. Do not turn work.

Row 5: With M ch3, dc to end, ch3, turn.

Row 6: dc to end, do not turn work but bring up the contrasting yarn by looping it through the back side of the M stitches of rows 5 and 6.

Row 7: [This fabric has a right side. The quadruple tr are hooked at the back of the work—the back being the right side.] * Quadruple tr hooked into the back of the second st of the previous C row, 3dc, rep from * to last 3sts, 1 quadruple tr hooked into previous C row, 2dc. Join in M, ch3, turn. Rows 2–7 form the 6-row pattern.

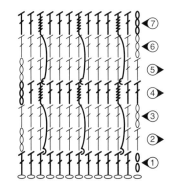

Smooth Wave Stitch

This two-color stripe pattern uses two different stitches to create curves. Try a piece with 29ch in M.

Row 1: 1sc in 3rd st from hook, 2sc, *4dc, 4sc, rep from * to end, turn.

Row 2: Ch1, 3sc, *4dc, 4sc (the dc should sit on dc and sc on sc), rep from * to end changing to C in last st, turn.

Row 3: Ch3, 3dc, *4sc, 4dc, rep from * to end.

Row 4: As row 3 changing to M in last st, turn.

Rows 5 and 6: as row 2.

Rep rows 3–6 to desired length.

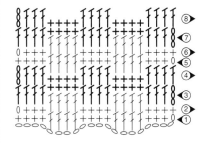

Dribble Stitch

Dribble stitch breaks up the stripe by "dribbling" into its own color on a previous row—one long stitch is inserted into the row below the one being worked. Using two colors, try a piece with 26ch, in M.

Row 1: 1sc in 2nd ch from hook, 1sc, ★ch1, skip 1ch, 3sc, rep from ★ to last 3sts, ch1, skip 1ch, 2sc, ch3, turn.

Row 2: 1dc, ★ch1, skip 1ch, 3dc, rep from ★ to last 3sts, ch1, skip 1ch, 2dc changing color in last st, ch1, turn.

Row 3: 2sc, 1tr in skipped ch on previous sc row, ★1sc, ch1, skip 1 st, 1sc, 1tr in skipped ch on previous sc row, rep from ★ to last 2sts, 2sc, ch3, turn.

Row 4: 3dc, ch1, skip 1ch, 3dc, rep from ★ to last st, 1dc changing color in last st, ch1, turn.

Row 5: 2sc, ch1, skip 1st, ★1sc, 1tr in skipped ch on previous sc row, 1sc, ch1, skip 1 st, rep from ★ to last 2sts, 2sc, ch3, turn.

Rows 2–5 form the pattern; rep these rows to desired length.

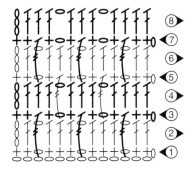

Spike Stitch

Spike stitch changes the look of a broad stripe of color into geometrical patterns, thus removing the straight look of a stripe. Try working a trial piece of spike stitch, starting with the main color (M) and 25ch (or a multiple of 4 + 1).

Row 1: 1sc in 3rd ch from hook, sc to end, ch1, turn.

Work 5 rows sc, change to C.

Row 7: Ch1 [acts as first sc], 1sc in st 2 rows below, 1sc in st 3 rows below, 1sc in st 4 rows below, ★ 1sc, 1sc in st 2 rows below, 1sc in st 3 rows below, 1sc in st 4 rows below, rep from ★ to end, ch1, turn.

Work 3 rows sc, change to M. Repeat last 4 rows, changing color after every 4 rows. By varying the number of rows in which to place the hook, you can form many different geometric patterns.

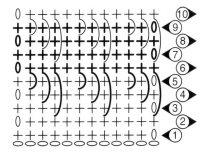

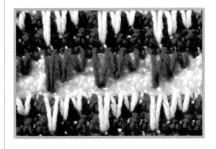

Polka-dot Stitch

Polka-dot stitch is a more elaborate way than seed stitch of producing spots of color. Make a trial piece with 25ch, starting with the main color.

Row 1: 1dc in 4th ch from hook, ch3, 1sl st in first ch, 2dc in same place as first dc, ★skip 6ch, (3dc, 1p, ch1, 1dc, 1p, 2dc) all in next st, rep from ★ to last 7ch, (3dc, 1p, 1dc) in last ch, join in C, ch3, turn.

Row 2: 1 hdc in same place, ★(hdc ch2 hdc) in 1ch sp of fan, ch3, rep from ★ to last shell, 2hdc in top of turning ch on row 1. Do not turn work.

Row 3: In M ch3, (1dc, 1p, 2dc) in 1 ch sp, ★(3dc, 1p, ch1, 1dc, 1p, 2dc) in next 3ch sp, rep from ★ to end, (3dc, 1p, 1dc) in top of turning ch, change to C, ch3, turn. Rep rows 2 and 3 for the desired length.

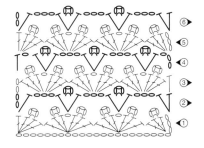

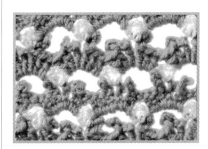

Project 4: Bathroom Rug

Crocheted bands of color in varying stitch combinations create this colorful rug. You may find that the gauge varies as you move from band to band, so try one of the simple alternatives if you are not yet experienced at maintaining the correct gauge.

Materials

Sport-weight cotton yarn, approx. 300yd. (280m.) in Cream (A)
Approx. 150yd. (140m.) of the same in each of Beige (B), Lilac (C), and Yellow (I)
Approx. 75yd. (70m.) of the same in each of Magenta (D), Red (E), Oyster (F), Pink (G), Lemon (H), Dusty Pink (J), Salmon (K), and Purple (L)
Size G/6 and H/8 (4.50mm and 5.00mm) hooks

Size

19½ x 32in. (50 x 92cm.)

Gauge

8sts and 7 rows to 2in. (5cm.) worked over sc with smaller hook

To Make

Ch81 in A.
Row 1: 1dc in 4th ch from hook, 1dc in each ch to end, join in B.
Row 2: (no turning chain) ★ 1dc, sl st, rep from ★ to end (79sts). Do not turn work.
Row 3: Insert hook into first st of row 2. With A ch3, dc to end changing to B in last st, ch1, turn.
Row 4: In front lp of st only, sc to end. Do not turn.
Row 5: Insert hook into first st of row 2. With A 3ch, 1dc in each back lp of row 3 to end, changing to B in last st (this leaves row 4 resting on top of row 5), ch3, turn.
Row 6: dc to end, changing to B in last st. No turning chain; turn.
Rep rows 2–6 once.
Rep rows 2 and 3 once more joining in C in the last st, ch1, turn. Fasten off A and B.
Row 14: sc to end, ch1, turn.

Rep row 14 3 times, joining in D in the last st, 1ch, turn.
Row 18: Work in spike stitch as follows: ★1sc in row below, 1sc 2 rows below, 1sc 3 rows below (top of previous color band), 1sc 2 rows below, 1sc 1 row below, 1sc, rep from ★ 12 times, ch1, turn.
Rep row 14 3 times joining in C in the last st by slipping the yarn up the side of the D rows. Fasten off D.
Row 22: As row 18 in C, joining in E in the last st, ch1, turn. Fasten off C.
Rep row 14 twice omitting ch1 at end of last rep and joining in F, working ch2 in F, and a further ch1 in G, turn.
Row 25: ★With G work 1dc changing to F as st is completed, with F work 1dc changing to G as st is completed, rep from ★ to end (the last st should be in F). Do not turn work.
Row 26: Insert hook into first st and with E ch1, sc to end, changing to G in last st, ch2 in G, ch1 in F, turn.
Row 27: ★With F work 1dc changing to G as st is completed, with G work 1dc changing to F as st is completed, rep from ★ to end (the last st should be in F). Do not turn work. Fasten off F and G.
Row 28: Insert hook into first st and with E ch1, sc to end, ch1, turn.
Row 29: As row 14 changing to H for ch1, turn.
Row 30: As row 14 but with ch2 to turn.
Row 31: Change to larger hook. Take colors I, J, and K together, laying all 3 strands across the top of previous row so that they are ready to be crocheted over. The sc is worked over the strands, trapping them inside the st. Skip 1 st, ★1sc over 3-color strands, ch1, skip 1 st, rep from ★ to end, ch2, turn. Constant attention should be made to ensure that strands lie loosely and do not act as a drawstring to the work.
Rep row 31 6 times, working ch1 to turn on the last row. Fasten off I, J, and K.
Change to smaller hook. Work row 14 twice joining in C in the last st, ch1, turn. Fasten off H.
Rep row 14 twice joining in F in the last st, ch1, turn. Fasten off C.

Row 42: Join in E to work a second turning chain, *1sc changing to F as st is completed, 1sc changing to E as st is completed, rep from * to last st, 1sc in F, ch1, turn.

Row 43: *1sc changing to E as st is completed, 1sc changing to F as st is completed, rep from * to last st, 1sc in E, ch1, turn.

Rep rows 42 and 43 once joining in C in last st, ch1, turn. Fasten off F and E.

Rep row 14 twice omitting turning ch and changing to A in last st, ch3, turn.

Row 48: dc to end, join in B.

Rep rows 2–8 joining in L in last st.

Rep row 14 twice omitting ch1 at end of last rep and joining in A, working ch2 in A and a further ch1 in C, turn.

Row 57: *With C work 1dc changing to A as st is completed, with A work 1dc changing to C as st is completed, rep from * to end.

Row 58: *With A work 1dc changing to C as st is completed, with C work 1dc changing to A as st is completed, rep from * to end changing to L in last st.

Rep row 14 twice changing to G in the last st.

Rep row 14 twice but end with ch2 and change to larger hook.

Row 63: Worked as row 31 using colors D, E, and H as the strands that G will trap.

Rep row 63 twice more. These last 3 rows are the central band of the rug.

Change to smaller hook and reverse the whole pattern.

To Complete

Very neatly and carefully darn in all the ends. This is not an easy rug to edge, so the way the ends are incorporated needs to follow the colors of the rug design itself.

Fringe both ends of the rug using cut lengths of yarn 5in. (10cm.) long in colors A and B.

SIMPLE ALTERNATIVES

Try making a complete rug using the stitch pattern from just one band of the striped rug. The following stitch patterns are listed in order of difficulty, starting with the easiest.

• *First band (rows 1–13) in bee st using colors A and B.*

• *Second band (rows 14–21) in spike stitch using colors C and D.*

• *Fifth band (rows 41–47) using sc in alternating colors E and F. This band is edged in sc with C.*

• *Seventh band (rows 55–60) using dc in alternating colors C and A. This band is edged in dc with L.*

• *Third band (rows 22–29) using dc in alternating colors G and F broken by one row sc in E with broader bands of E.*

• *Eighth band (rows 61–67) can be worked with only 3 rows trapping the 3 colors, followed by stripes of G and L .*

• *Fourth band (rows 30–38) is the most difficult for maintaining the correct gauge and needs constant checking. It can be worked as an overall pattern, but each row must be checked to ensure that the strands being trapped have not gathered the crochet.*

Project 5: Square Pillow Cover

This striped, three-color pillow cover is made from the combination of single and double crochet. It is perfect for practicing adding different-colored yarns, as the color changes at the end of each row.

Materials

Sport-weight cotton yarn, approx. 150yd. (140m.) in Pink (A) and Purple (C)
Approx. 75yd. (70m.) of the same in Oyster (B)
Size G6 (4.50mm) hook
6 buttons
pillow form size 14 x 14in. (35 x 35cm.)

Size

The pillow cover is smaller in width and length than the pillow form by approximately 1in. (2.5cm.).

Gauge

10sts to 2½in. (6.5cm.); 1 patt rep of 6 rows to 2in. (5cm.)

To Make

Ch 53 in A.
Row 1: 1dc in 4th ch from hook, 1dc, ★5sc, 5dc, rep from ★ to end finishing with 3dc, ch3, turn (51sts).
Row 2: 2dc, ★ 5sc, 5dc, rep from ★ to end finishing with 3dc and changing to B in last st, ch1, turn.
Row 3: sc to end changing to C in last st, ch1, turn.
Row 4: 2sc, ★ 5dc, 5sc, rep from ★ to end finishing with 3sc, ch1, turn.
Row 5: as row 4 changing to B in last st, ch1, turn.
Row 6: as row 3 changing to A in last st, ch3, turn.
Row 7: 2dc, ★ 5sc, 5dc, rep from ★ to end finishing with 3dc, ch3, turn.
Rows 2–7 form the pattern. Rep these rows until twice the length of

the pillow cover has been reached.
Work 1 more pattern of 6 rows.
Last row: in A ch1, skip 1 st, 1dc, ★5sc, 2dc, ch1, skip 1 st, 2dc, rep from ★ to end finishing with 1dc, ch1, skip 1 st, 1dc. Fasten off.

To Complete

Fold the rectangle so that the buttonhole edge overlaps the beginning of the work by one pattern repeat. Join the side seams of the cover on the inside, either by sewing or by working sc through both pieces. Sew on the buttons to match the buttonholes. Insert the pillow form; close.

CHAPTER FOUR

Shaping Workshop

T HERE ARE TWO MAIN METHODS of shaping in crochet. One is by either increasing or decreasing, and the other is to make use of different stitch heights. Because the crochet hook sits on top of the stitches, it is possible to vary the height of each stitch without changing the size of the crochet hook itself.

Putting increases in the centre of rows creates peaks which make the rest of the work slope downward. Conversely, decreasing creates dips which pull the fabric upward on either side. Multiple increases can be used to create circles, which are dealt with in more detail in the workshop on motifs and circles on pages 98–117. Increasing and decreasing within one row or over two rows can produce a variety of pattern designs such as the circles in the Catherine Wheel on page 59.

To perfect your increasing and decreasng skills, try crocheting lots of different diamond or triangle shapes in the same size but using different yarns.

Increasing

It is easier to increase than to decrease in crochet. All you need to do is add a stitch by placing another stitch in the same place as the one just worked. At the beginning of a row, you place your hook in the tiny hole just to the left of the turning chain and before the next stitch. At the end of a row, place two stitches in the top of the turning chain of the previous row. This applies to any size of stitch from single crochet upward. (Any increasing required within a lacy or complex pattern will be calculated and described for you.)

Increasing by more than one stitch at the side(s) of the work will require the addition of chains. (You need to do this, for example, when working a sleeve that is made in one piece with the bodice.) Adding enough chains at the end of the previous row for both the new foundation chain and the extra number of stitches is easy: after the last stitch, work one chain for each additional stitch required, plus the turning chain. The length of chain is then worked into in precisely the same way as any row beginning with a starting chain. Once the extension is finished, continue across the stitches until you reach the last

stitch. If you were to add a new length of chain as described above, the second extension would be one row higher than the first. Instead, remove the hook from the row in progress (a few temporary chains will prevent unraveling), take a new length of yarn, and attach this yarn to the top of the last stitch of the previous row (see the diagram below). Crochet a length of chain of the number required, but without the addition of turning chain. Fasten off the extra yarn. Return to the interrupted row and continue by working over the new extension. In this way you are sure that one side matches the other.

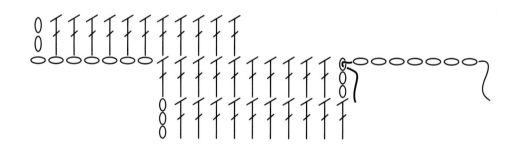

Adding multiple stitches

Decreasing

Older patterns may tell you to decrease by working slip stitch along to the next stitch at the beginning of the row and to stop before the last stitch at the end of the row. Unfortunately, this produces a stepped effect, rather than a curve. Decreasing and increasing should produce smooth diagonal or curved edges.

For most stitches the method of decreasing is to draw together two stitches at the top so that on the next row there is only one stitch to work into. Begin the first of the two stitches as usual, but stop when two loops still remain on the hook. Now work the second stitch until there are three loops on the hook, then put the yarn over the hook and draw it through all three loops. This method does not leave holes or create steps. The diagram below shows a double-crochet decrease (dc2tog).

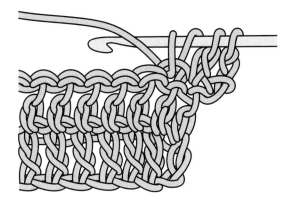

Decreasing A Half Double

The half double stitch is unusual in that it is completed by drawing the yarn through three loops rather than two, as in other stitches. Therefore the general method for decreasing cannot apply. Instead, work the first stitch at the beginning of the row as an unfinished single crochet, and the second stitch as an unfinished half double, then pull the yarn through four loops to complete. At the end of the row, work the penultimate stitch as an unfinished half double and the last stitch as an unfinished single crochet, completing the decrease by pulling the yarn through four loops.

Practical Exercise: Making A Diamond

Work this diamond pattern to become familiar with both increasing and decreasing.
Ch4.
Row 1: 2dc in 4th ch from hook (beg of ch), ch3, turn (3 sts).
Row 2: 1dc in same place as turning ch, 1dc, 2dc in last st, ch3, turn (5 sts).
Row 3: 1dc in same place as turning ch, dc to last st, 2dc in last st, ch3, turn.
Increase row: Repeat row 3 to the halfway measure of the diamond. This increases each row by 2sts.
Decrease row: dc2tog, dc to last 2sts, dc2tog, ch3 turn. This decreases the row by 2sts.
Repeat the above row until 5 sts rem.
Next row: (dc2tog) twice, ch3, turn.
Last row: dc2tog.

This is what your crochet diamond should look like.

Decreasing Within A Row

Not all patterns are worked from bottom to top. To allow for draping and ease of completion, with an attractive edge, it may be necessary to work from the top down. Another way to work is from side to side, so that the rows run vertically, not horizontally.

Occasionally it is necessary to work shaping all along a row, particularly when one edge of the article is shorter than the other—for example, a lampshade cover where the top is narrower than the base, or a sleeve or skirt with a pattern that is worked around the arm or the body.

Decreasing using stitch heights is a wonderful way of shaping along rows. Work a row in double crochet until you reach the point for the shaping. Work one-third of the remaining length in half double, the next third in single crochet, and the remainder in slip stitch to take you to the end of the row, ready to start the return row. The result is a wedge or long dart effect. This method is also ideal for including darts in awkward shapes.

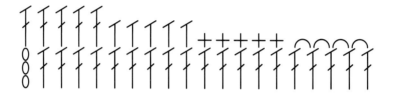

Shaping by stitch height

Corners

*Corners can be rounded, in which case ordinary increasing is sufficient. However,
if you want a sharp, angular corner, follow the instructions in the tip box.*

To achieve a right angle in double crochet at an outer corner, you need to work three stitches into one, with the second stitch forming the point of the corner (see the diagram below). Corners worked in other stitches will take fewer stitches if shorter, more stitches if taller.

To determine how many more or fewer stitches need to be calculated, think of the corner as a curve where the outer edge is part of the circumference of a circle. Use a table of stitch heights from the information given on page 103 to enable you to do this.

When working an inner corner (such as a square neck) which requires a decrease rather than an increase, a double-crochet cluster would give an accurate result, keeping the two edges at right angles.

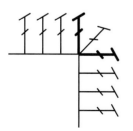

Three corner stitches

TIP

The central stitch in an outer corner may need to be longer than the other stitches if a sharp point, rather than a slightly curved corner, is required. For example, use a triple instead of a double crochet if you think the original result is not precise enough.

Stitch Library

Increase your repertoire of stitches by trying these stitch patterns, which use both varied stitch heights and increasing/decreasing in a row.

Fleur-De-Lys

This pattern allows two colors to integrate with each other. The work is turned every two rows. Try a piece starting with 27 chains.

Special abbreviations:

1RclF—Leave the last lp of all sts on hook—1RdcF around next dc, skip 1ch, 1dc in top of next sc, skip 1ch, 1RdcF around next dc, (4 lps on hook), yo and pull through all 4 lps.

1RclB—Made as 1RclF but inserting hook around the back of the stitches in the cluster.

Row 1: (RS) In M 1dc in 4th ch from hook, *ch1, skip 2ch, 1sc, ch1, skip 2ch, ** 3dc in next ch, rep from * ending last rep at **, 2dc in last ch. Do not turn work.

Row 2: (RS) Join C at beg of row, ch1, 1sc in same place, *ch2, 1RclF, ch2, 1sc in next dc, rep from * to end, turn work.

Row 3: (WS) With M ch3, 1dc in same place, *ch1, skip 2ch, 1sc in next cl, ch1, skip 2ch,** 3dc in next sc, rep from * ending last rep at **, 2dc in last sc. Do not turn.

Row 4: (WS) In C ch1, 1sc in same place, *ch2, 1RclF, ch2, 1sc in next dc, rep from * to end, turn.

Row 5: (WS) In M ch3, 1dc in same place, *ch1, skip 2ch, 1sc in next cl, ch1, skip 2ch,** 3dc in next sc, rep from * ending last rep at **, 2dc in last sc. Do not turn.

Rep rows 2–5 to desired length.

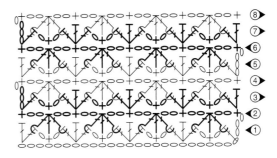

Chevrons

Ch24 (or a multiple of 10 + 4)

Row 1: 1dc in 4th ch from hook, *3dc, dc3tog, 3dc, 3dc in next ch, rep from * to end but finishing with only 2dc in last st, ch3, turn.

Row 2: 1dc in same place as turning ch, *3dc, dc3tog, 3dc, 3dc in next st, rep from * to end but finishing with only 2dc in last st.

Check that the 3dc in one stitch sits in the center of each 3dc group and that the dc3tog has the dc3tog in its center, from the row below.

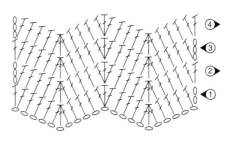

Long Wave Stitch

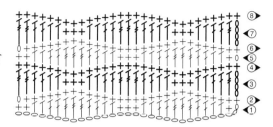

By varying the height of the stitches, you can change the shape of a stripe. Two colors emphasize the look of the pattern. Change color on every alternate row. Try a piece using 30 chains.

Row 1: (RS) place first st in 3rd ch from hook, ★1sc, 2hdc, 2dc, 3tr, 2dc, 2hdc, 2sc, ★rep from ★ to end, ch1, turn.

Row 2: sc to end, change color in last st, ch 4, turn.

Row 3: ★1tr, 2dc, 2hdc, 3sc, 2hdc, 2dc, 2tr, rep from ★ to end, ch1, turn.

Row 4: As row 2.

Row 5: ★1sc, 2hdc, 2dc, 3tr, 2dc, 2hdc, 2dsc, ★rep from ★ to end, ch1, turn.

Row 6: As row 2.

Rep rows 3–6 to desired length.

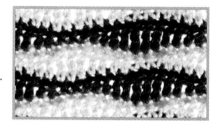

Violet

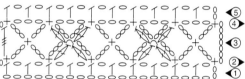

This lacy pattern uses clusters to produce a petal effect. This trial piece is worked on 31 chains.

Row 1: 1hdc in 5th ch from hook, ★ch1, skip 1ch, 1dc in next ch, rep from ★ to end, ch1, turn.

Row 2: 1sc in same place ★ch6, skip 1hdc, 1sc in next hdc, ch3, 2dcl in same st, skip 1hdc, 2dcl in next st, ch3, 1sc in same place as cl, rep from ★ to last 2sps, ch6, 1sc in last st, ch7, turn.

Row 3: 1sc in 6ch sp, ch3, ★2dcl, ch3, sl st, ch3, 2dcl all in center of next dcl gr, ch3, 1sc in next 6ch sp, ch3, rep from ★ to end, 1dtr in last st, ch1, turn.

Row 4: ch1, 1sc in same place, ★ch3, 1sc in top of cl, rep from ★ to last 7ch, 1sc in 3rd ch from sc in 6ch sp, ch3, turn.

Row 5: 1hdc in 3ch sp, (ch1, 1hdc) in sc, ch1, rep from ★ to end. (Note: the last chain is for turning.)

Rep rows 2–5 to desired length.

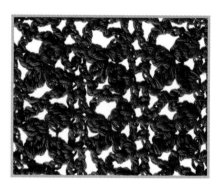

Boat

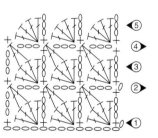

This stitch creates a "rocking boat" pattern. Try a piece starting with 26 chains.

Special abbreviation: dcl—Yo, insert hook into st, yo, draw yarn through to front, yo, draw through 2 lps, yo, insert hook into next st, yo, draw through to front, yo, draw through 2 lps, draw through all 3 lps.

Row 1: 1sc in 3rd ch from hook, ★ch3, 4dc in same ch as sc, skip 3ch, 1sc in next ch, rep from ★ to end, ch3, turn.

Row 2: ★skip 1dc, 2dcl over 2dc, ch3, skip 1dc, 1sc in top of 3ch, rep from ★ to end, ch1, turn.

Row 3: 1sc in same place, ★ch3, 4dc in same place, 1sc in next, rep from ★ to end, ch3, turn.

Rep rows 2 and 3 to desired length.

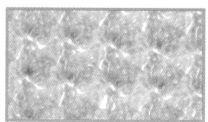

Catherine Wheel

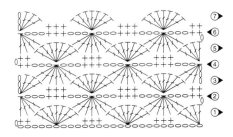

The circular motifs are achieved by working one row of clusters and one row of shells. Try a piece starting with 27 chains.

Row 1: (WS) 1sc in 2nd ch from hook, 1sc in next ch, ★skip 3ch, 7dc in next ch, skip 3ch, 3sc, rep from ★ to last 4ch, skip 3ch, 4dc in last ch, turn.

Row 2: ch1, 1sc in same place, 1sc, ★ch3, 1dcl worked over 7sts, ch3, 3sc, rep from ★ to last 4sts, ch3, 1cl over 4dc, turn.

Row 3: ch3, 3dc in same place, ★skip 3ch, 3sc, skip 3ch, 7dc in loop of cl, rep from ★ to last 5sts, skip 3ch, 2sc, turn.

Row 4: ch3, 1cl over 3sts, ★ch3, 3sc, ch3, 1cl over 7 sts, rep from ★ to last 5sts, ch3, 2sc, turn.

Row 5: ch1, 2sc, ★skip 3ch, 7dc in loop of cl, skip 3ch, 3sc, rep from ★ to last st, 4dc in last st.

Rep rows 2–5 to desired length.

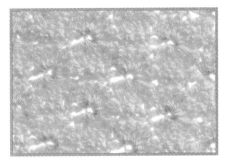

Two-color Catherine Wheel

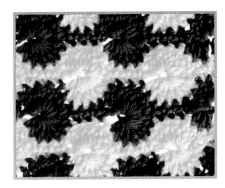

Work as above, changing to the second color on row 2.
Change color on every alternate row.

Egg

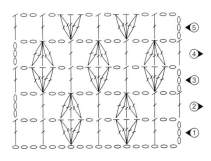

Another way of using shells and clusters to form a pattern. Try starting with 29 chains.

Row 1: 1dc in 8th ch from hook, ★ch1, skip 2ch, (dc2tog, 1dc dc2tog) in next ch, ch1, skip 2ch, 1dc in next ch, rep from ★ to end, ch5, turn.

Row 2: 1dc in next dc, ch2, ★(5 dcl made by placing 2dc in 2dcl 1dc in dc and 2dc in 2dcl), ch2, 1dc in next dc, ch2, rep from ★ to end placing 1dc in last st, ch4, turn.

Row 3: ★(dc2tog, 1dc, dc2tog) in next dc, ch1, skip 2ch, 1dc in 5dcl, ch1, rep from ★ to end omitting last ch and placing 1dc in 3rd of 5ch, ch5, turn.

Row 4: ★5dcl, ch2, 1dc in next dc, ch2, rep from ★ omitting 2ch at end of last rep, 1dc in 3rd of 4ch, ch5, turn.

Row 5: 1dc in 5dcl, ★ch1, 1dc in 5dcl, ch1, 1dc in 5dcl, rep from ★ to last dc, ch2, 1dc in 3rd of 5ch.

Project 6: Tweed Mittens

These classic adult's mittens are crocheted in counterpane stitch with a turned-back cuff.
The child's mittens are worked in single crochet and you could even make a simple crochet cord to
attach to the mittens so that they aren't dropped or lost.

Adult's Mittens

Materials

1 50g. (1¾oz.) ball of Rowan Felted Tweed in Melody (M)
1 50g. (1¾oz.) ball of Rowan Felted Tweed in Corn (C)
Size F/5 and G/6 (4.00mm and 4.50mm) hooks

Size

One size (average woman's hand)

Gauge

12sts to 3¼in. (8cm.) 4 rows to 2in. (5cm.)

Special Abbreviation:

cp—Counterpane stitch (insert hook into st, yo, draw through to front, yo, pull through 1 lp only, yo, draw through both lps on hook).

Hand

With larger hook ch14 in M.
Row 1: 1cp in 4th ch from hook, cp to end, 2ch, turn.
Row 2: 1cp in same place as turning ch, 4cp, (2cp in next st) twice, 4cp, 2cp in last st, ch2, turn.
Row 3: 1cp in same place as turning ch, 6cp, (2cp in next st) twice, 6cp, 2cp in last st, ch2, turn.
Row 4: 1cp in same place as turning ch, 8cp, (2cp in next st) twice, 8cp, 2cp in last st, ch2, turn.
Row 5: cp to end, ch2, turn (24 sts).
Row 6: 1cp in same place as turning ch, 10cp, (2cp in next st) twice, 10cp, 2cp in last st, ch2, turn.
Row 7: As row 5 (28 sts).
Rep row 7 20 times.

Cuff

Change to smaller hook and C.
Row 1: ch1, sc to end, ch1, turn.
Row 2: sc to end, ch1, turn.
Rep row 2 4 times. Change to larger hook.
Rep row 2 6 times. Do not break off yarn.

Buttonhole Tab

Row 1: Place 5sc in the rows worked with the larger hook (the turning ch makes it 6 sts), ch1, turn.
Row 2: 5sc, ch1, turn.
Row 3: 3sc, sc2tog, ch1, turn.
Row 4: 1sc, ch1, skip 1 st, 2sc, ch1, turn.
Row 5: 3sc, fasten off.

Thumb

Ch4 with larger hook and M.
Row 1: 2dc in 4th ch from hook, ch2, turn.
Row 2: 1cp in same place as turning ch, 2cp in next st, 1cp, ch2, turn.
Row 3: 1cp in same place as turning ch, 1cp, 2cp in next st, 2cp, ch2, turn.
Row 4: 1cp in same place as turning ch, 2cp, 2cp in next st, 3cp, ch2, turn.
Row 5: 1cp in same place as turning ch, 3cp, 2cp in next st, 4cp, ch2, turn.
Row 6: 1cp in same place as turning ch, 4cp, 2cp in next st, 5cp, ch2, turn.
Row 7: cp to end, ch2, turn.
Rep row 7 4 times.
Row 12: sc2tog, 2cp, (sc2tog) twice, 2cp, sc2tog, ch1, turn.
Row 13: ★sc2tog, rep from ★ to end, fasten off.

To Complete

Join the top of the mitten and 16 rows down to thumb insertion.

Join the thumb from the tip to the first row of cp without an increase.

Insert the thumb shaping into the seam of the hand, stretching the thumb edge slightly to fit the hand piece. Work from the base of the thumb downward on one side.

Repeat on the other side of the thumb and mitten.

Continue to join the seam.

Change color for joining the cuff. Incorporate the turn-back of the cuff that does not have the buttonhole tab into the side seam. Sew on the button.

Complete the other mitten to match, remembering to reverse all seams so that there is a right and a left hand.

Child's Mittens

Materials

1 50g. (1¾oz.) ball of Rowan Felted Tweed in Willow (M)
1 50g. (1¾oz.) ball of Rowan Felted Tweed in Crush (C)
Size E/4, F/5, and G/6 (3.50mm, 4.00mm, and 4.50mm) hooks

Size

To fit the hand of a 3–5 year-old child

Gauge

9 sts and 11 rows to 2in. (5cm.)

Hand

With medim-sized hook ch14 in M.
Work rows 1–7 as for hand of adults mitten, substituting sc for cp throughout.
Rep row 7 17 times.

Cuff

Change to smallest hook and C. Ch7.
Row 1: 1sc in 3rd ch from hook, 4sc, sl st to next st of hand, 1sl st in next st of hand, turn.
Row 2: 1sc in back lp only to end, ch1, turn.

Row 3: 1sc in back lp only to end, sl st to next st of hand, sl st in next st of hand, turn.
Rep rows 2 and 3 until all the sts of the hand have been used.

Thumb

With medium-size hook and M ch3.
Row 1: 2sc in 3rd ch from hook, ch1, turn.
Row 2: 1sc in same place as turning ch, 1sc in next st, 2sc in last st, ch1, turn.
Row 3: 1sc in same place as turning ch, 5sc 2sc in last st, ch1, turn.
Row 4: 1sc in same place as turning ch, 7sc, 2sc in last st, ch1, turn.
Row 5: sc to end, ch1, turn.
Rep row 5 7 times.
Row 13: ★sc2tog, rep from ★ to end, fasten off.

To Complete

Join the thumb from the tip to the first row without an increase.

The beginning of the thumb shaping sits at the point where the cuff begins. Measure where the shaping ends and mark on the seam of the mitten.

Join the top and seam of the mitten to the point of thumb shaping insertion.

Insert the shaped part of the thumb into the seam of the hand, stretching the thumb edge slightly as it is joined to the hand piece.

Change color for joining the cuff.

Both mittens are the same.

Optional: Make a cord long enough to stretch easily down both sleeves and across the child's back. For a simple, attractive cord, make a chain using 6 strands of yarn and a size H/8 (5.50mm) hook. This will have a rope-like effect.

SIMPLE ALTERNATIVES
• *The cuff of the adult's mitten could be worked with a raised double crochet rib (see page 69).*
• *The child's mitten can be turned into a baby's mitten by stopping the increasing at row 4 (24 sts), working fewer rows, and omitting the thumb.*

Project 7: Camisole

This stylish camisole is an excellent project for practicing your shaping skills. It is worked downward from the neck, beginning with the shaped triangular pieces which hold the shoulder straps. An interesting use of picots creates a delightful braid-like strap.

Materials

Size 20 tightly spun, mercerized crochet cotton in Lilac: approx. 425yd. (390m.) for 30in. bust; 566yd. (520m.) for 32, 34, and 36in. bust; and approx. 708yd. (650m.) for 38in. bust
Size B/1 (2.00mm) hook

Size

To fit 30(32,34/36,38) in. [76(81,86/91, 96)cm.] bust.
Length of back from neck edge to base: 15in. (38cm.)

Gauge

15 sts and 10 rows to 2in. (5cm.)

Triangles (work 4 alike)

Row 1: (RS) Ch4, 2dc in first ch made, ch1, turn (3 sts).
Row 2: 1sc in same place as turning ch, 1sc, 2sc in last st, ch3, turn (5 sts).
Row 3: 2dc in same place as turning ch, 1dc, ch1, skip 1 st, 1dc, 3dc in last st, ch2, turn (9 sts).
Row 4: 2sc in same place as turning ch, 7sc, (2sc 1hdc) all in last st, ch4, turn (13 sts).
Row 5: (1tr 1dc) all in same place as turning ch, ch1, skip 1 st, 9dc, 1ch, skip 1 st, 1dc 2tr in last st, ch2 turn (17 sts).
Row 6: 1sc in same place as turning ch, 15sc, (1sc 1hdc) all in last st, ch4, turn (19 sts).

Row 7: (1tr 1dc) all in same place as turning ch,★ 8dc, ch1, skip 1 st, dc to last st, 1dc 2tr in last st, ch2 turn (23 sts).
Row 8: 1sc in same place as turning ch, 21sc, (1sc 1hdc) all in last st, ch4, turn (25 sts).

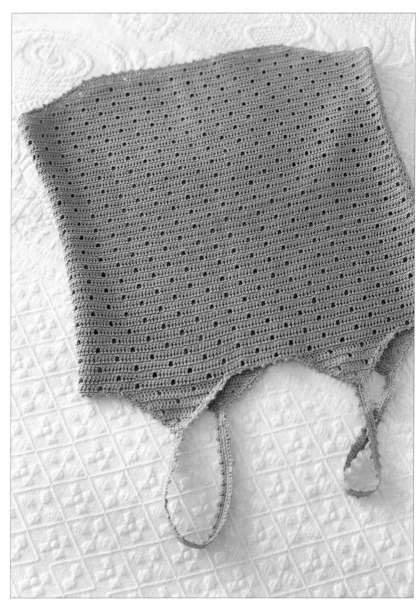

Row 9: (1tr 1dc) all in same place as turning ch, 6dc, *ch1, skip 1 st, 9dc, rep from * once, ch1, skip 1st, 6dc, 1dc 2tr in last st, ch2 turn (29 sts).
Fasten off.

Body (work 2 alike)

It is important to make sure that the wrong side of each triangle faces you as you incorporate it into the body of the camisole.
Row 1: (RS) Ch18(18,28,28), 29sc over first triangle (all sts used), ch21(21,21,31), 29sc over second triangle, ch20(20,30,30).
Row 2: (WS) 1dc in 4th ch from hook, *ch1, skip 1 st, 9dc, rep from * to last 3 sts, ch1, skip 1 st, 2dc, ch1, turn.
Row 3: sc to end, ch3, turn.
Row 4: 6dc, *ch1, skip 1 st, 9dc, rep from * to last 8 sts, ch1, skip 1 st, 7dc, ch1, turn [95(105,125,135) sts].
Row 5: As row 3.
Row 6: 1dc, *ch1, skip 1 st, 9dc, rep from * to last 3 sts, ch1, skip 1 st, 2dc, ch1, turn.
Rep rows 3–6 until work measures 9¼in. (23cm.) from center point of neck.
Increase 1 st at each end of every alternate dc row (i.e. every 4th row) for 20 rows, keeping sequence of eyelet pattern. End with an sc row [115(125,145, 155] sts).

Base Of Body

Row 1: Sl st across 5 sts, 1sc, 1hdc, keeping patt sequence dc to last 7 sts, 1hdc, 1sc, 1sl st, turn.
Row 2: (no turning chain) sl st to first sc, 1sc in each dc, sl st in hdc, turn.
Rep rows 1 and 2 4 times Fasten off.
Work another side the same.
Join both side seams.

Shoulder Straps

Ch78 from center of a triangle on one side of the body and connect to the opposite triangle on the other side of the body. 1sc in each ch to end picking up 2 strands of thread, sl st to triangle, return down the strap on the opposite side inserting hook into sc over the chain. Fasten off.

Edging The Armhole

Rejoin yarn to center underarm *3sc, ch2 sl st in sc just made, rep from * to end to include shoulder strap, join to beg with sl st. Work other armhole the same.

Edging The Neck

Join yarn to center back neck and work as for armhole using front and back neck stitches plus both shoulder straps.

Edging The Base

Join at side seam and work edging around front and back joining with sl st to fasten off.

CHAPTER FIVE

Textured Stitches Workshop

To QUOTE TEXTILE ARTIST Jan Messent, "Texture should be able to be felt by a blind person but a pattern can exist within a fabric without being felt." This is a textbook definition of "texture" for general design, but texture can also describe a fabric or yarn that has a composition of uneven strands of yarn or a rough surface. "Textured yarns" are usually novelty yarns incorporating slubs, knops, mohair strands, bouclé loops, etc., whereas textured fabric normally refers to a fabric with a nubby, lumpy, bumpy kind of texture created by the stitches.

This workshop deals with creating texture by using raised stitches or by drawing multiple stitches together. You can give a fabric a heavy texture of ridges and valleys by inserting your hook around the stem, or "post," of a stitch and moving the stitch forward or backward. Using this technique and incorporating longer stitches to allow them to cross over each other will result in a heavy cable or twisted rope effect. You can then place a few popcorns or bobbles between the columns of cables to imitate Aran, or fisherman, sweater designs.

Raised Stitches

One way to obtain texture is to work raised stitches, pushing a stitch either forward or backward to create an "embossed" style of pattern. Simply insert the hook to the right of the stitch, then take it across the stitch to emerge at the left-hand side of the same stitch. Raised stitches can be of any length.

Raised Double Crochet (Post Stitch)

Doubles are very suitable for introducing texture into a crochet fabric. Taking the hook around the stem of a stitch—often called "working around the post"—will either lift it forward or push it backward. Bobbles, clusters, popcorns, and puff stitches produce an embossed look and feel in a fabric. All these stitches are created by putting groups of stitches in the same place and then counting them as only one stitch.

Raised doubles or triples produce fabrics similar to those in traditional knitted British and Irish fisherman' sweaters. These are worked while making the fabric and not as surface crochet afterward. There is a way of working an Aran style of crochet by using surface chains after the article is completed, employing a method similar to tambour chain stitch. However, in my opinion this limits the amount of texture you can achieve, and therefore I am happier using raised crochet stitches.

On the whole, crochet should not use more yarn than knitting, and this also applies to Aran-style crochet. Knitted Aran sweaters are much heavier than stockinette-stitch sweaters, and equally crocheted Aran-style sweaters are heavier than other fabrics, as it is the nature of the design. It should be remembered, when ordering or buying yarn to make raised double crochet designs, that the pattern is likely to take a little more yarn than required for other crochet pattern designs.

Raised Double Crochet Front (RdcF) *(2 ch to turn)*

Since this is a double crochet, you would expect to use three chains to lift the hook to the top of the stitch. But because you place the hook into the work around the stem of the stitch and not in the top, you need two chains only to lift it. RdcF stitch will pull the fabric toward you, which is why it is referred to as a raised double front. It does not mean it will be on the right side of the fabric automatically, only pushed forward.

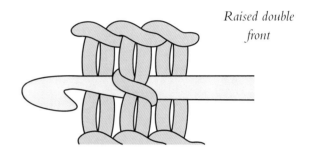

Raised double front

To make a raised double front: Yo, insert hook from right to left around stem of st below, yo, draw hook from behind stem (3 lps now on hook), ★yo, draw through 2 lps, rep from ★ once.

Raised Double Back (RdcB) *(2 ch to turn)*

RdcB pushes the stitch away from you and therefore is referred to as a raised double back.

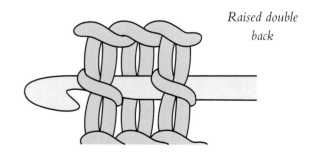

Raised double back

Work in a similar way as for a RdcF, but insert the hook from right to left around the stem of the double from behind the fabric. The working of the stitch will push the stem of the double to the back.

Raised Double Rib

You can make an elasticized waistband or cuff by using raised doubles. The chain from which the first row of doubles is made *is not elastic*, so all ribs must be worked outward from the main fabric. The elasticity of the stitch fabric or rib becomes more pronounced as the rows are completed.

Insert the hook this way to push the stitch to the front.

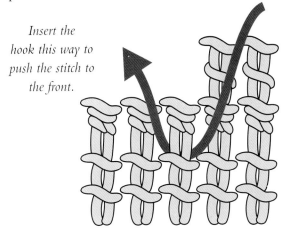

Insert the hook this way to push the stitch to the back.

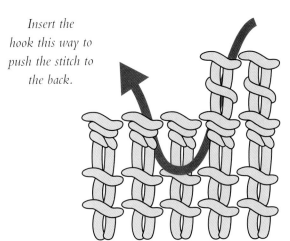

Make a chain with an equal number of stitches, plus 2.
Row 1: 1dc in 4th ch from hook, 1dc in each st to end, ch2, turn.
Row 2: ★1RdcF, 1RdcB, rep from ★ to last st, place a Rdc round last st by inserting hook into the space in whatever direction comes next, ch2, turn.
Row 3: Look at the stitches on row 2 once the work has been turned to decide whether the next st is pushed back or forward. If back, begin with a RdcB; if forward, begin with a RdcF. Keep all Rdc in a continuous line.
Repeat until a sufficient length has been made.

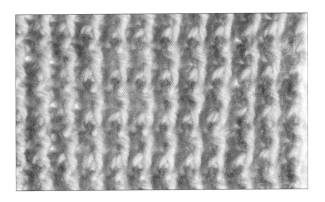

An example of a piece of raised double rib crochet

Cables

Most cable effects are worked in a background of doubles or occasionally half doubles. By just following the pattern, you can obtain a narrow, simple cable effect, over two stitches. Unfortunately, when crossing two or more stitches over each other, you will find holes appearing between the columns of ordinary stitches and the cable effects. To avoid this, add a "ghost" stitch (see below). It is unusual to find a crochet cable pattern that includes ghost stitches. However, once you have learned the technique you can apply it to any pattern where you are unhappy with the result because of a gap occurring between stitches.

Ghost Stitches

In a base row of double crochet make a ghost stitch by working one unfinished treble in the next stitch (this stitch will not be counted). Work the first raised stitch as written in the pattern of cable of double triple on page 74, leaving the last loop of the stitch on the hook. Yarn over hook and draw through all three loops. Continue with the rest of the cable of double triple pattern as given, leaving the last of the stitches in the cable pattern unfinished (two loops on the hook). Make a second ghost stitch by working an unfinished double in the top of the stitch around which the previous raised stitch was worked (three loops on the hook), yarn over hook and draw through all three loops. The cable stitch patterns in the stitch library (see pages 73-74) are given as ordinary pattern instructions. *It is up to you* to improve on both these patterns, and any others you may see, using the techniques of ghost stitches.

Clusters

The term "cluster" is given to several stitches that are drawn together at the top. Throughout this book all stitches gathered together at the top will be a "cluster," whether the stitches sit as a group in one stitch at the bottom or are spread over a number of stitches. You will have found several stitch patterns in the Shaping Workshop that use this technique primarily to form inverted shells. Clusters can flatten with use, particularly when worked in soft acrylic and wool yarns. Clusters are more accentuated if they are worked with the wrong side of the fabric facing. A standard 3dc cluster (3dcl) requires the number of turning chains to be the same as the height of the stitch between the clusters: a 3dcl put into an sc row requires only one chain, a 3dcl put in a dc row requires three chains. When a cluster is placed in a row of short stitches, it is more pronounced than when it is placed in a row of stitches the same height as the cluster.

1 For a 3dcl, the stitches can be placed either in the same place or (as shown above) using 3 consecutive stitches. Yo, insert hook into the fifth chain from the hook, yo and pull through to the front, yo and pull through 2 loops (2 loops on the hook).

2 Yo, insert hook into the stitch, yo and pull through to the front, yo and pull through 2 loops (3 loops on the hook).

3 Repeat step 2 once. At this point there are 4 loops on the hook.

4 Yo and pull through all 4 loops (3dcl completed). This is also a method of decreasing.

Popcorns

Puff stitch is the easiest of the stitches with a "wraparound" look. Unlike clusters, popcorns retain their texture even after pressing. This method of making a popcorn brings it to the front. If you want it at the back, insert the hook from back to front.

1 Have the right side of the crochet facing. Place 4–6dc into the same stitch, depending on how pronounced you want your popcorn to be.

2 Remove the hook from the stitch and insert it from front to back of the first of the 6dc just made.

3 Collect the loose loop and pull it through to the front. Continue crocheting along the row in the usual way.

There are two variations to the working of popcorns:
a) Add ch1 after the popcorn is made, to ensure that no stitches are lost on the return row. I am not sure that this is a sensible method, for it may create too many stitches in the next row and may also change the appearance of the fabric, depending upon the yarn and which stitches follow;
b) Work the popcorn in a row of shorter stitches such as sc or hdc. This produces a larger bump than when working in a row of double crochet.

71

Puff Stitch

This method of making several stitches out of one produces a smoothly rounded bump on the surface of the fabric. Basically, a puff stitch consists of a collection of double crochet stitches worked in the same stitch of the previous row then joined by a yarn-over and, often, by an additional chain stitch.

1 Yo, insert the hook into the stitch, yo and pull a loop through, lift the hook to a horizontal position so that the loop coming through the stitch is elongated.

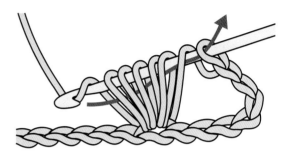

2 Pull through 2 more long loops. Yo, pull through all 7 loops on hook.

3 Work an extra chain to close the puff stitch firmly (optional). On the following row, remember to work only into one of the two chains, so as to avoid adding stitches.

The puff stitch is much more effective if worked in rows of shorter stitches. If you cannot place puff stitches into rows of short stitches, you may need to work the instructions in steps 1 and 2, 4, 5, or even 6 times, depending upon the thickness of the yarn.

Bobbles

One of the difficulties in crochet is the lack of standardization of stitch names. A "bobble" is rarely the name of a stitch unless the designer of a particular pattern has decided to give this name to a formation of stitches. Bobbles can be popcorns, puff stitches, clusters, or even a long double in a short-stitch row!

Stitch Library

Combining columns of some of the stitch patterns in this workshop will allow you to simulate knitted Aran, or fisherman, patterns.

Cable Of Triple Over 2 Stitches (tr2 cable)

This is one of the smallest cable patterns and requires a multiple of 4 chains, plus 2.

Row 1: 1dc in 4th ch from hook, 1dc in each ch to end. ch2, turn.

Row 2: *skip 1 st, 1RtrF in next st, 1RtrF in st just skipped, 2dc, rep from * to last 3sts, skip 1 st, 1RtrF in next st, 1RtrF in st just skipped, 1dc, ch2, turn.

Row 3: * 2RdcB, 2dc, rep from * to last 3sts, 2RdcB, 1dc, ch2, turn. Rep rows 2 and 3 to the desired length.

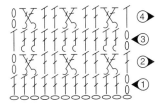

Bouclé Stitch

Bouclé stitch pushes the taller triple stitch away from the crochet worker and therefore should be worked with the wrong side facing. Begin with 27 chains.

Row 1: 1dc in 4th ch from hook, dc to end, ch1, turn.

Row 2: *1tr, 1sc to end, ch3, turn.

Row 3: dc to end, ch1, turn. Rep rows 2 and 3 to the desired length.

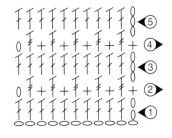

Diamonds Made Of Open-leg Raised Dc Clusters

Special abbreviation:
RclF—For ease of writing a special abbreviation RclF has been included in the pattern. This is made by working all the raised trebles into the double crochet rows.
This is a good design for creating a waffle effect and it makes a fabric with an attractive texture.

Begin with 25 chains.

Row 1: 1sc in 3rd ch from hook, sc to end, ch3, turn (24 sts).

Row 2: dc to end, ch1, turn.

Row 3: 1RtrF around 3rd sc of first row (4th st), * 3sc, 1 unfinished RtrF around same st of first row (2 loops on hook) skip 3sc on row 1, 1 unfinished RtrF in next sc (3 loops on hook) yo and draw through all 3 loops—1RclF made—rep from * to last 3 sts, 3sc, ch3, turn.

Row 4: dc to end, ch1, turn.

Row 5: 2sc, *1RclF, 3sc, rep from * to last st, 1sc, 3ch, turn. From row 5 all Rtr are worked around the stems of previous Rtr. Rep rows 2–5 until you have the desired length .

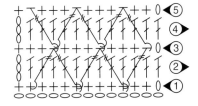

Popcorn Columns

The jagged columns of dc popcorns are separated by a line of raised doubles. Begin with 27ch.
Row 1: 1dc in 4th ch from hook, dc to end, ch3, turn.
Row 2: 1dc, ★1RdcF, 1dc, 1 popcorn to lie at front of work, 2dc, rep from ★ to last 3sts, 1RdcF, 2dc, ch3, turn.
Row 3: 1dc, ★1RdcB, 1dc, 1 popcorn to lie at back of work, 2dc, rep from ★ to last 3sts, 1RdcB, 2dc, ch3, turn.
Rep rows 2 and 3 to the desired length.

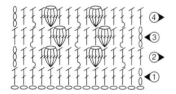

Cable Of Double Triple Over 4 Stitches (dtr 4 cable)

A slightly wider cable using a multiple of 6 chains, plus 4. Remember to add the ghost stitches at start and end of cables on row 2. Begin with 28 chains.
Row 1: 1dc in 4th ch from hook, 1dc in each ch to end, ch2, turn.
Row 2: 1dc, ★ skip 2 sts, 2RdtrF, 2RdtrF in 2 sts just skipped, 2dc, rep from ★ to end.
Row 3: 1dc, ★4RdcB, 2dc, ch2, turn.

Rep rows 2 and 3 to the desired length.

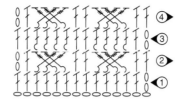

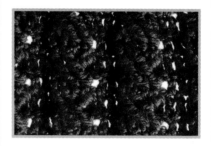

Basket Weave

Basket weave is created by a 2 by 2 raised double stitch pattern. In this instance the raised stitches do not form columns but give a woven effect as in basket making. Begin with 28 chains (or any multiple of 4).
Row 1: 2dc in 4th ch from hook, 1dc in each ch to end, ch2, turn (26 sts).
Row 2: 1RdcF, ★2RdcB, 2RdcF, rep from ★ to end, ch2, turn.
Rep row 2 to desired length.

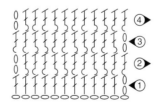

Puffs

A simple fabric looks very different when puff stitches (see page 72) have been incorporated. Try this with 29 chains.
Row 1: 1dc in 4th ch from hook, ch1, turn.
Row 2: ★1 puff st, 3sc, rep from ★ to last 2 sts, 1 puff st, 1sc, ch3, turn.
Row 3: dc to end, ch1, turn.
Row 4: sc to end, ch3, turn.
Row 5: as row 3.
Rep rows 2–5 to desired length.

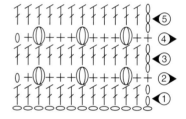

Project 8: Simple Aran Sweaters

These adult's and child's sweater projects in classic Aran designs allow you to practice the cabling techniques you have learned in this workshop.

Adult's Sweater

Materials

24(30,36) 50g. (1¾oz.) balls of Rowan DK Cotton in Rusty Orange
Size G/6 and H/8 (4.50mm and 5.00mm) hooks

Size

To fit: 30-32(34-36, 38-40)in. [76-81(86-91, 96-102)cm.] bust/chest
Actual size: 36(42,48)in. [90(105,120)cm.] bust/chest

Gauge

7sts and 6 rows to 2in. (5cm.)

Special Instructions

cable to Front—Skip 2 sts 2RtrF, 2RtrF in skipped sts going in front of last 2 sts 2RdcF
cable to Back—Skip 2 sts 2RtrB, 2RtrB in skipped sts going behind last 2 sts 2RdcB
cable 4 Front—Skip next 2 sts, 2RtrF in next 2 sts, 2RtrF in skipped sts going in front of last 2 sts
cable 4 Back—1RdcB in next 4 sts

Back

With larger hook ch65(73,81).
Foundation row: This row forms the first row of the body and the first row of the waistband when working the raised double rib. 1dc in 4th ch from hook, dc to end, ch1, turn (63[71,79] sts).
Row 2: sc to end, ch3, turn.
Row 3: dc to end, ch1, turn.
Rep these 2 rows until work measures 23in. (58cm.). Place a marker in 17th(20th,23rd) st from each end leaving 29(31,33) sts in the center. Fasten off.

Front

With larger hook ch82(92,102).
Foundation row: This row forms the first row of the body and the first row of the waistband when working the raised double rib. 1dc in 4th ch from hook, dc to end, ch1, turn (80[90,100] sts).
Row 2: 7(12,17)hdc ★1RdcF, 1RdcB, cable 4 Front, 1RdcB★ rep from ★ to ★ 8 times, 1RdcF, 8(13,18)hdc, ch2, turn.
Row 3: 7(12,17)hdc ★1RdcB, 1RdcF, cable 4 Back, 1RdcF★ rep from ★ to ★ 8 times, 1RdcB, 8(13,18)hdc, ch2, turn.
Rep these 2 rows until work measures 20in. (50cm.) ending with a wrong side row.

Divide for Neck—First Side

Row 1: Patt over 30(35,40) sts, dec 1 st over the next 2 sts (this is with 1hdc and 1sc drawn tog), turn.
Row 2: Sl st into next st, dec 1 st over the next 2 sts (this is with 1sc and 1hdc drawn tog), patt to end, ch2, turn.
Row 3: Patt over 27(32,37) sts, dec 1 st over the next 2 sts, turn.
Row 4: As row 2.
Row 5: Patt over 24(29,34) sts, dec 1 st over the next 2 sts, turn.
Row 6: As row 2.
Row 7: Patt over 21(26,31) sts, dec 1 st over the next 2 sts, ch2, turn.
Cont straight on these sts until work measures 27in. (69cm.). Fasten off.
Note: 1¼in. (3cm.) of these last rows go over the top of shoulder to join the back. With right side facing skip 14 sts, rejoin yarn in next st.

Second Side

Row 1: Dec 1 st over the next 2 sts (this is with 1sc and 1hdc drawn tog), patt to end, ch2, turn.

Row 2: Patt over 29(34,39) sts, dec 1 st over the next 2 sts (this is with 1hdc and 1sc drawn tog), turn.

Row 3: Sl st into next st, dec 1 st over the next 2 sts, patt to end, ch2, turn.

Row 4: Patt over 26(31,36) sts, dec 1 st over the next 2 sts, turn.

Row 5: As row 3.

Row 6: Patt over 23(28,33) sts, dec 1 st over the next 2 sts, turn.

Row 7: As row 3.

Cont straight on these sts until work measures 27in. (69cm.). Fasten off.

Sleeves

With larger hook ch47.

Foundation row: This row forms the first row of the sleeve and the first row of the cuff when working the raised double rib. 1dc in 4th ch from hook, dc to end, ch2, turn (45 sts).

Row 2: 12hdc 1RdcF, 1RdcB, cable 4 Front, 1RdcB, 1RdcF, 3hdc, 1RdcF, 1RdcB, cable 4 Front, 1RdcB, 1RdcF, 13hdc, ch2, turn.

Row 3: (WS) 12hdc, 1RdcB, 1RdcF, cable 4 Back, 1RdcF,1RdcB, 3hdc, 1RdcB, 1RdcF, cable 4 Back, 1RdcF, 1RdcB, 13hdc, ch2, turn.

Row 4: As row 2.

Row 5: Keep patt straight, but increase 1 st at beg and end of row.

Cont increasing on WS rows for another 14(16,18) inc. (This gives 28[32,36] rows 75[83,91] sts.)

Work without increases until the sleeve measures 16in. (41cm.).

Cuff

Decrease 4(2,0) sts evenly while working the first row of the cuff.

Row 1: Rejoin yarn to bottom of sleeve with RS facing and smaller hook, work the sts round the stems of the dcs in the Foundation Row. Ch2, 1RdcF in same place as turning ch, *1RdcB, 1RdcF, rep from * to end, ch2, turn (48sts).

Row 2: *1RdcF, 1RdcB, rep from * to end, ch2, turn. Rep Row 2 5 times.

Fasten off.

Waistband

Join 1 side seam, leaving an opening large enough to insert the sleeve.

Row 1: With RS facing and smaller hook, rejoin yarn to bottom of sweater. Work the sts around the stems of the dcs in the Foundation Row. Ch2, *1RdcB, 1RdcF, rep from * to end, ch2, turn. *You require an even number of sts.*

Row 2: *1RdcF, 1RdcB, rep from * to end, ch2, turn. Rep row 2 6 times. Fasten off.

To Assemble

Join other side seam, shoulder seams, and sleeve seams; set in the sleeves.

Neck

Row 1: With RS facing and smaller hook, join yarn to center back neck. Ch2, hdc to corner, hdc evenly down side of neck to unworked sts on front, hdc across centre sts, hdc evenly up second side, hdc across sts to center back, join to top of 2ch with sl st, ch2, turn.

Row 2: Check you have an even number of sts. *1RdcF, 1RdcB, rep from * to end, ch2, turn. Rep row 2 3 times. Fasten off.

To Complete

Join top of sleeve to body, checking you have the same number of rows from the waistband at front and back. Join sleeve and side seams.

Child's Sweater

Materials

9(10,10,11) 50g. (1¾oz.) balls of Rowan 4-ply Cotton in Red
Size G/6 and H/8 (4.50mm and 5.00mm) hooks
4 buttons

Size

To fit: 20(22,24,26)in.[51(56,61,66)cm.] chest
Actual size: 24(26,28,30)in. [61(66,71,76)cm.] chest

Gauge

7 sts and 6 rows to 2in. (5cm.) worked in half double

Special Instructions

As adult sweater

Back

Using smaller hook ch46(48,50,52).
Row 1: Work sc in each ch (45[47,49,51] sts).
Row 2: sc to end, ch1, turn.
Rep row 2 twice.
Row 5: As row 2, ch2, turn.
Row 6: 3(4,5,6)dc, ★2dc in next st, 5dc, rep from ★ 5 times, 2dc in next st, 4(5,6,7)dc, ch2, turn [52(54, 56,58) sts]. Change to larger hook.
Row 7: 7(8,9,10)hdc ★1RdcF, 1RdcB, cable 4 Front, 1RdcB★ rep from ★ to ★ 4 more times, 1RdcF, 8(9,10,11)hdc, ch2, turn.
Row 8: 7(8,9,10)hdc ★1RdcB, 1RdcF, cable 4 Back, 1RdcF★ rep from ★ to ★ 4 more times, 1RdcB, 8(9,10,11)hdc, ch2, turn.
Rep these 2 rows until work measures 13¾(14¼,15,15¼)in. [35(36,38,39)cm.]. (††)
Change to smaller hook. Work 3 rows in sc. Fasten off.

Front

Work as for Back but stop 6 rows below (††).

Neck Shaping (first side)

With WS facing patt 19(20,20,21) sts, dec 1 st over 2, ch2, turn. *Note: Substitute hdc for Rdc when dec.*
Dec 1 st at neck edge on next 4(4,5,6) rows (14[15,14,14]sts).
Work straight until work measures the same as back. Fasten off.

Neck Shaping (second side)

With WS facing skip 10(10,12,12) sts, rejoin yarn, ch2, dec 1 st over next 2 sts, patt to end.
Dec 1 st at neck edge on next 4(4,5,6) rows (14[15,14,14] sts).
Work straight as back. *Do not break off yarn.*

Neck Band

Change to smaller hook. sc across shoulders around neck (dec at corners of neck) and other shoulder, for 2 rows. Mark 1 buttonhole on each shoulder 1 st from neck edge, and a second buttonhole 4 sts along.
Last Row: sc to end replacing 1sc with ch1 when you reach the marker.
Fasten off.

Sleeves

Ch22(22,24,24) with smaller hook.
Row 1: 1 sc in 3rd ch from hook, sc to end, ch3, turn. Work 3 rows in sc (21[21,23,23] sts).
Row 5: 1(1,2,2)dc, ★2dc in next st, 3dc, rep from ★ 3 times, 2dc in next st, 2(2,3,3)dc, ch2, turn [25(25,27,27)dc].
Change to larger hook.
Row 6: 1(1,2,2)hdc ★1RdcF, 1RdcB, cable 4 Front, 1RdcB★ rep from ★ to ★ twice more, 1RdcF, 2(2,3,3)hdc, ch2, turn.
Row 7: 1(1,2,2)hdc ★1RdcB, 1RdcF, cable 4 Back, 1RdcF★, rep from ★ to ★ twice more, 1RdcB, 2(2,3,3)hdc, ch2, turn.
Inc 1 st at each end of next and every alternate row until 50(52,54,56) sts.
Work straight until work measures 10½(11,11½,12¼)in. [27(28,29,31)cm.] or desired length. Fasten off.

To Complete

Join all pieces together overlapping front neck band at shoulders.

SIMPLE ALTERNATIVES
• *Work fewer cables, replacing them with hdc, to save yarn.*
• *Make into a vest by omitting the sleeves and waistband. Do not join the last 6in. (15cm.) at the base of the side seams. Replace waistband with 2 rows sc and 1 row crab st at armhole and waistband plus slits.*

Project 9: Baby's Blanket

Create a soft, cotton baby's blanket in contrasting sections of textured stitches. A feature of this blanket is the edging that has been incorporated as a trim. Edgings can stand proud from a fabric to create a heavier texture.

Materials

7 1¾oz. (50g.) balls of Rowan Cotton Glacé in Ecru
Size F/5 (4.00mm) hook

Size

19 x 24in. (48 x 61cm.)

Gauge

10 sts and 6 rows to 2in. (5cm.)

Special Instructions

1psc—nsert hook as for an sc, yo, draw through to front (2 lps on hook), ch3 through first lp, complete as an sc.

Special Instructions (continued)

Rtr2tog—Note that in this instance there are 3 sts separating the tr before being joined tog.

Center Panel (make one for the central strip)

Ch20.

Row 1: 1sc in 3rd ch from hook, 1psc *psc, 3sc, rep from * to end, ch3, turn (19 sts).

Row 2: dc to end, ch1, turn.

Row 3: 1psc, 1sc, 1Rtr2tog working first tr around 2nd sc of previous sc row, skip 3 sts on previous sc row and working second tr around next sc. 1sc in next st, 1psc, 1sc, *1Rtr2tog working first tr around same sc worked for previous Rtr2tog, skip 3 sts on previous sc row and working second tr around next sc. 1sc in next st, 1psc, 1sc, rep from * to end, ch3, turn.

Row 4: As row 2.

Row 5: 1Rtr around 4th sc of previous row, *1sc in next st, 1psc, 1sc, 1Rtr2tog, rep from * to last 5 sts, 1sc in next st, 1psc, 1sc, 1Rtr around sc used for last Rtr2tog, 1sc, ch3, turn.

Rep rows 2–5 until work measures 22½in. (57cm.) ending with an sc row.

Center Of Side Pieces
(make two for the outside strips)

Work exactly as above until work measures 7½in. (19cm.) finishing with an sc row. Fasten off.

Edging For Center Side Piece

Row 1: ch1, 28sc, ch4, turn.

Row 2: 1tr in same place as turning ch, 1dc, 1hdc, 1sc, *ch3, 1tr in same place as sc, 1dc, 1hdc, 1sc, rep from * to end. Fasten off.

Work other side the same.

Corner Pieces (make 4)

Ch38.

Row 1: 1hdc in 4th ch from hook, dc to end, ch2, turn (36 sts).

Row 2: 1RdcF, 2RdcB, 2RdcF, rep from * to end, ch2, turn.

Rep row 2 until work measures 8½in. (21cm.). Fasten off.

Note: the groups of 2 raised stitches alternate front and back to form a basketweave.

To Complete

Attach center side piece foundation edge between two corner pieces by sewing the edging in such a way as to allow the points to stand free.

Sew the three panels together.

Work an edging as for the central side pieces around all four sides.

ALTERNATIVE IDEAS

• Work the blanket in two colors.

• Add a braid along the central strips and at the edge of the blanket.

• Work just one of the patterns for a one-pattern design.

• Increase the size of the blanket for a buggy cover or for a crib.

CHAPTER SIX

Tunisian Crochet Workshop

Tunisian crochet has a variety of other names, including afghan stitch and *tricot écossais* ("Scottish knitting"), but in spite of all these names, it did not develop in Tunisia, Scotland, or Afghanistan.

Tunisian crochet is worked on a long hook called an afghan hook, which looks like a cross between a crochet hook and a knitting needle. Flexible afghan hooks are also available, and these look like an ordinary crochet hook with a plastic wire attached. The end of the wire contains a movable stopper so that the stitches do not slip and drag the weight of the work out of shape.

The fabric Tunisian crochet produces is not unlike a woven textile. It appears to be a cross between knitting and weaving, and the actions used to make it are a mixture of these two crafts. The crochet loops are picked up in one direction, as though picking up stitches in knitting, and then crocheted off in the other direction.

Tunisian Crochet

Tunisian crochet does not contradict the principle that all crochet starts and ends with a loop on the hook. It, too, starts with a slip knot, followed by a chain.

The Tunisian row involves picking up the loops in one direction and removing them in another direction to leave just one loop on the hook. A word of warning: when reading Tunisian crochet patterns, check how the designer has written the instructions—some designers describe the picking up and taking off of the loops as one row of basic Tunisian stitch, while others describe the process as two rows. This book counts the picking up and taking off of the loops as one row.

The Right Side Of Tunisian Work

Unlike the main form of crochet, in which the two sides of the work are usually identical, Tunisian crochet has a right and a wrong side and is generally worked with the right side facing you. In most Tunisian stitches this is the side with the short vertical strands. The back of the fabric looks like the rough side of an ordinary knitted fabric. This is true even when textured stitches are being worked, except when the Tunisian hook is being used to make a fabric that looks like the "rough" or purl side of knitting.

Following Tunisian Patterns

Even if only basic stitches are being used it is useful to look and see if you can change the pattern to get a better finish. For instance, more than one pattern piece can be worked together to avoid seams. Before beginning, simply add the number of chains required for all the pieces to be worked. Because Tunisian crochet does not require additional chains, even for turning, the sum of the chains is the numbers required to work your first row. This technique is particularly suitable for cardigans, jackets, edge-to-edge vests, etc.

COMMON PROBLEMS AND HOW TO SOLVE THEM

Problem: *The work leaning, particularly slanting to the right.*
Action: *Check that you are going into the second vertical strand and not using the first strand.*
Action: *Check that you are picking up the vertical strand at the front of the fabric and not going through the work from front to back.*

Problem: *Insufficient stitches. That is, losing stitches on each row.*
Action: *Check that you are picking up the last strand (see step 7 on page 86).*
Action: *Check that you are picking up the vertical strands and not the horizontal strands.*

Problem: *Lack of height: although the gauge is correct widthwise, there are insufficient rows to provide the length required.*
Action: *The hook should sit on top of the work when you pick up the loops. Frequently the hook is allowed to sit in front of the last row, which shortens the loops on the hook and in turn shortens the work, making it a denser fabric which uses more yarn than is necessary.*

TIP
Because the right side is facing at all times, this stitch is particularly suitable for people who can use only one hand: the hook can be placed in a waistband, belt, or clamp.

Basic Tunisian Stitch (Ts)

Using a crochet hook one size smaller than the afghan hook, make a chain with the same number of stitches as are required for the Tunisian pattern. Change to the afghan hook.

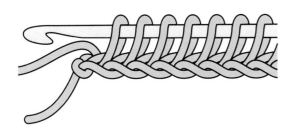

1 Insert the hook into the second chain, picking up the top strand of the chain only, yo, *draw through, insert the hook into the top of the next chain, yo, draw through, repeat from * to end. You should have 1 loop on the hook for each chain worked. It is easier to count the number of stitches now, before you have completed all the steps.

2 Yo, pull through 1 loop—this is the equivalent of 1 turning chain, which raises the hook into the correct position.

3 *Yarn over, pull through 2 loops.

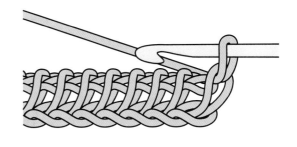

4 Repeat from * to end of row.

This row makes a base from which to start a basic Tunisian stitch fabric. Some patterns refer to the row worked into the chain as the foundation row or rows, so read your pattern carefully and make sure that you can count your rows correctly.

The action of picking up loops on one row and taking them off on another creates a vertical strand at the front of the work once the first row has been

completed. Pick up the vertical strand in front of the stitches for the next row of loops. This is rather like picking up stitches to make a row of knitting, and, in fact, if you are a knitter you will find that knitting principles apply on the pick-up rows.

5 No turning chain is made at the start of the pick-up procedure. The loop on the hook is the first stitch of the row. Insert the hook into the next strand.

6 *Yarn over hook.

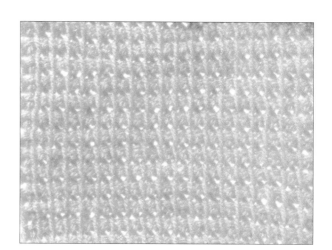

7 Pull loop through to the front, repeat from * in step 6 until all vertical strands have been used, including the one at the end. Complete the row with 1 chain and remove the loops as for the first row.

An example of basic Tunisian stitch

Increasing

To increase at the start of the row you should follow the method below.

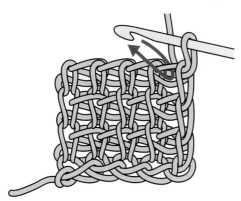

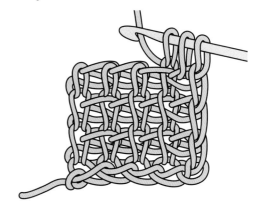

1 Insert the hook under the horizontal strand lying between the loop on the hook and the next stitch.

2 Before picking up the next vertical strand, yo, and pull through in the usual way. Continue in basic Tunisian stitch. To increase at any other point, pick up the horizontal strand lying between the stitch just worked and the next stitch.

Decreasing

There are different methods of decreasing, but I find this one to be the easiest.

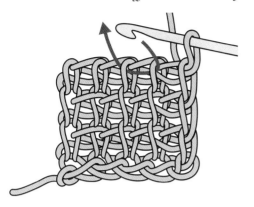

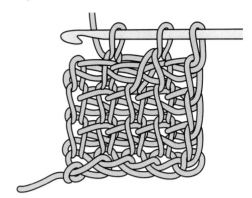

1 Decrease on the pick-up row by inserting the hook under 2 vertical strands at the same time.

2 Yo, pull the yarn through both strands at once, leaving only 1 loop on the hook for the 2 stitches. To make decreases look symmetrical within the same piece of fabric, work the decreases 2 or 3 stitches from each end.

Joining Yarn And Changing Color

Always leave enough of the last yarn used to sew into the loops at the back of the work. Then pull the new yarn through, leaving enough yarn to sew in the opposite direction at the back of the work.

Joining In A New Yarn

Straight-edged stripes are formed when a new color is joined in at the end of the take-off action,

when there are only two loops left on the hook. Joining it at this point also avoids a color drag.

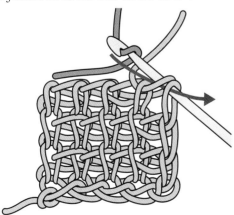

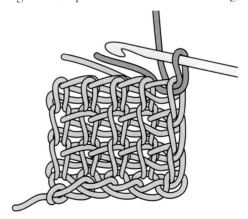

1 When 2 loops remain on the hook, yo in a new color.

2 Draw the new yarn through both loops.

Creating A Tweed Effect

The "tweed" effect is achieved when a new color is joined halfway through the row. When all the loops have been picked up in one direction, join in a new color, yo, draw through one loop, ★yo, draw through two loops, repeat from ★ to end. Return with the second color. Once all the loops have been picked up with this second color, pick up the first color to take off all the loops once more. Once again, return with the color being worked. Each time you have returned and all the loops are on the hook, change color. One color is being pulled

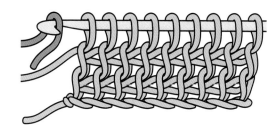

Joining in a new color to be blended with that on the hook

through another on each row, which means that there is no color drag or any long loops to take care of.

Finishing Basic Tunisian Stitch

Because basic Tunisian stitch is a solid fabric, it is important to avoid introducing holes when finishing the work. The following methods will show you how to do this. It is necessary to insert the small hook as you would the Tunisian hook.

The Last Row

To work the last row, use an ordinary crochet hook, two sizes smaller than the size of afghan hook used. Continue to pick up only the vertical strand at the front of the work and make one single crochet in every strand to the end.

  IMPORTANT: Pick up as usual for basic Tunisian stitch, but work a full single crochet leaving no loops on the hook. Do not go through the work as in an ordinary single crochet fabric.

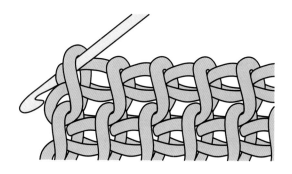

Picking up at the edge

Side Borders

Working a single crochet border into the sides of the Tunisian fabric needs extra attention to avoid making holes on one side. This is because the right-hand side looks like normal crochet chains which can be worked in single crochet as usual, but the other side has only one strand of yarn to be worked into. Therefore the horizontal and the single loose strand need to be picked up and worked together.

Other Tunisian Techniques

Although it might seem that picking up so many loops first is more restrictive than ordinary crochet, it still allows for lots of innovation, as the hook has more directional freedom.

Tunisian Double Crochet (Tdc)

One chain is required at the start of the row to give the work the necessary lift and stop the sides from puckering, because this stitch has more height. Wrap the yarn over the hook once, then insert into the vertical strand, yo, pull through vertical strand, yo, pull through two loops *(do not repeat this process as you would in ordinary crochet or there will be no loops left on the hook for the next process)*. Continue in this way to the end of the row. Remove the loops as for basic Tunisian stitch.

Tunisian Treble (Ttr)

Make two chains at start of row, yo twice, and insert hook as for basic Tunisian stitch (yo, pull through two loops) twice, leaving the last loop on the hook. Remove loops as for basic Tunisian stitch.

Invisible Joins

To join the shoulders or any other seams invisibly, place the right side of one piece of Tunisian to the right side of the other piece of fabric *before any single* crochet has been worked, i.e. before finishing. Each stitch should match exactly the stitches of the other piece of fabric. Using a crochet hook smaller than the afghan hook, work one single crochet through the vertical strand of the fabric facing you and the vertical strand of the fabric away from you.

Buttonholes

To make a buttonhole in basic Tunisian stitch, work one chain, followed by yo, draw through three loops, when taking off the stitches, followed by one chain. Remove the loops as for the basic Tunisian stitch.

Stitch Library

Lacy and very dense fabrics can be obtained with an afghan hook. Experiment for yourself, or try working some of the stitch patterns below. As with ordinary crochet, Tunisian crochet can be worked with any type of yarn, so do experiment.

Tunisian Knit Stitch

This trial piece was worked on bulky yarn using a size 13 (9.00mm) hook for stitch definition—a larger hook is required for this stitch than for Ts. Make a trial piece with 18ch.

Row 1: Ts.

Row 2: *Insert hook through the fabric under the chains as shown in diagram below, yo and draw through, rep from * until 18 lps are on the hook, remove as for Ts.

Rep row 2 to desired length.

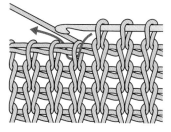

Insertion point for Tunisian knit stitch

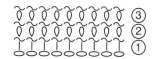

Pebble Stitch

Make a trial piece with 24ch, or any multiple of 2.

Row 1: Ts to end.

Row 2: The lp already on hook counts as the first st, pick up as for Ts. Return with ch1, yo, draw through 2 lps, *ch3, (yo, draw through 2 lps) twice, rep from * to end.

Row 3: Pick up as for Ts. Return with ch1, *(yo, draw through 2 lps) twice, ch3, rep from * to last 3 lps, (yo, draw through 2 lps) 3 times.

Rep rows 2 and 3 to desired length. Note that the crochet "pebbles" should not sit on top of each other.

Eyelet Stitch

Make a trial piece with 23ch, or any multiple of 2 + 1.

Row 1: Pick up 23 lps, ch2, yo and pull through 3 lps, *ch1, yo and pull through 3 lps, rep from * to end.

Row 2: (1 lp is already on hook) * pick up 1 lp from 1ch sp, pick up 1 lp out of ch, rep from * to end (23 sts), ch2, yo and pull through 3 lps, *ch1, yo and pull through 3 lps, rep from * to end.

Rep row 2 to desired length.

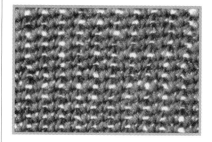

Tunisian Clusters

Try working a trial piece with 24ch, or any multiple of 4.

Special Abbreviation:

1Tcl—Yo, insert hook in vertical strand, yo, insert hook in same vertical strand, yo, draw through 5 lps.

Row 1: Ts.

Row 2: Pick up, remembering the lp on the hook is a stitch, 2Ts, ★1Tcl, 3Ts, rep from ★ to last lp, 1Ts, take off lps as for Ts.

Row 3: Pick up, ★1Tcl, 3Ts, rep from ★ to last 3 lps 1Tcl, 2Ts, take off lps as for Ts.

Rep rows 2–3 to desired length.

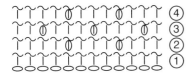

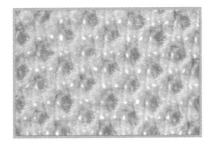

Claw Stitch

Claw stitch uses 2 colors. Make a trial piece with 25ch, or any multiple of 6 + 1, beginning in main color (M).

Rows 1–4: Ts changing to C in the last 2 lps of row 4.

Row 5: With C pick up 2 lps as Ts (not counting lp already on hook), ★1Ttr in vertical strand 3 rows below and 1 st back, 1Ttr in vertical strand 4 rows below, 1Ttr in vertical strand 3 rows below and 1 st forward, yo and draw through 3 lps, 5Ts, rep from ★ to last 4 sts, 1 3Ttr group, 3Ts, remove lps from hook as for Ts changing to M in the last 2 lps.

Rows 6–9: Ts changing to C in the last lps of row 4.

Row 10: With C ★pick up 5 lps as for Ts (not counting the lp already on hook), 1Ttr in vertical strand 3 rows below and 1 st back, 1Ttr in vertical strand 4 rows below, 1Ttr in vertical strand 3 rows below and 1 st forward, yo and draw through 3 lps, rep from ★ to last 6 sts, 6Ts, remove lps from hook as for Ts changing to M in the last 2 lps.

Repeat the pattern (rows 1–10) to desired length.

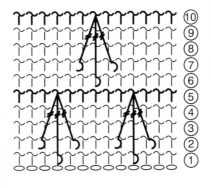

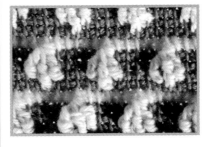

Roman Column

Make a trial piece with 23ch, or any multiple of 8 + 7, in contrasting color (C).

Row 1: Work 1Ts in each ch (23 sts), change to M.

Rows 2–3: In Ts changing to C at the end of row 3.

Row 4: 2Ts, ★ 1Ttr in previous C row skipping 2 sts (5th st in from edge), 1Ts (1 st of previous row not used), 1Ttr in first of 2 skipped sts in previous C row, 5Ts, rep from ★ to end finishing with 2Ts instead of 5Ts. Pull back in the usual way changing to M on last st.

Rows 2–4 form the pattern. Repeat these rows to the desired length.

Corded Stitch

For a slightly open look which accentuates the cord effect use a hook 2 sizes larger than you would for Ts. If you try this effect you may prefer the reverse side of the fabric. Alternatively, as this stitch is an adaptation of Tunisian knit stitch, revert to the normal size of Tunisian hook for a "knit stitch" look without the open effect.

Make a trial piece with 24ch.

Row 1: Ts.

Row 2: Ch1 to lift hook, ★insert hook as for Tunisian knit stitch, yo, draw through to front, yo, draw through 1 lp, rep from ★ until all lps are on hook, remove as for Ts.

Rep row 2 to desired length.

Project 10: Round Pillow

This round pillow is crocheted entirely in basic Tunisian stitch (see pages 85 and 86), working from the edge of the pillow to the center.

Materials

Sport-weight cotton yarn, approx. 75yd. (70m.) in each of petal color (A), petal edge color (C) and center color (D)
Approx. 380yd. (35 m.) of same in background color (B)
Size 7 (5.00mm) afghan hook
Size F/5 (4.00mm) crochet hook

Size

18in. (46cm.) in diameter

Gauge

8 sts and 8 rows to 2in. (5cm.)

To Make

Follow the instructions below to make one side of the pillow, then repeat to make the other side. If you want to make a plain circle for the back of the pillow, then follow the instructions in the simple alternative. Remember that when working in the round, short rows are used, and so it is sometimes necessary to leave some unworked loops on the hook to be used at a later stage.

Background

With D make a slip knot which tightens from the short end. Ch38.

Row 1: Pick up 38 lps. Take off as usual until 2 lps rem. (Remember that the first lp goes through only 1 st at the beginning of each row and is counted as 1 of the "take-off" lps.) Remove the 2 lps with C. Fasten off D, leaving 4in. (10cm.) for securing yarn.

Row 2: Pick up 18Ts (19 lps on hook), leaving rest of row 1 unworked. Take off until 2 lps are left. Remove the 2 lps with B. Fasten off C, leaving 4in. (10cm.) for securing yarn.

Row 3: Pick up 5Ts (6 lps on hook). Take off lps.

Row 4: With B pick up in Ts all color B sts plus 1 from row 2. Take off in B.

Rep row 4 9 times. (The last row leaves 3 unworked sts on row 2.)

Row 14: Still in B, pick up 14Ts (15 lps on hook). Take off in B.

Row 15: Pick up across the row leaving the last st of the previous row unworked. Take off.

Rep row 15 9 times. Do not break off yarn B; it will be attached until the pillow is complete. Keep 1B on hook.

Row 24: With C, pick up 5 sts from the last row, cont picking up 1 st from each of the unworked ends of the last 10 rows, plus 1 st from row 2 (17 lps on hook). Take off 15Ts (leaving 3 lps on hook—1B and 2C).

Row 25: With D, pick up 14Ts from row 24, 2Ts from row 2 and 2Ts from row 1. Take off 17Ts (this leaves 1B, 2C and 2D on the hook).

Row 26: With C, pick up 16Ts from row 25 plus 16 sts from row 1 leaving 1 st unworked. Take off 31Ts (7 lps still on hook—1B, 2C, 2D, 2C).

Petal

Row 1: In A, pick up 14Ts. Take off 3Ts (12 lps in A on hook).

Row 2: Pick up 2Ts and 2Ts from row 26. Take off 7Ts.

Row 3: Pick up 8Ts. Take off 11Ts.

Row 4: Pick up 12Ts. Take off 15Ts.

Row 5: Pick up 16Ts. Take off 19Ts.

Row 6: Pick up 20Ts. Take off 23Ts (leaving 1B, 2C, 2D, 2C and 2A on hook).

Row 7: Pick up 24Ts. Take off 23Ts.

Row 8: Pick up 20Ts. Take off 19Ts.

Row 9: Pick up 16Ts. Take off 15Ts.

Row 10: Pick up 12Ts. Take off 11Ts.

Row 11: Pick up 8Ts. Take off 7Ts.

Row 12: Pick up 4Ts. Take off 16Ts joining in C through the last 2 lps of A. (There are now 8 lps on the hook—1B, 2C, 2D, 3C.) The petal is completed. Cut A, leaving 4in. (10cm.) to fasten off securely.

Continue Background (row 26)

Row 27: With C, pick up 27Ts (35 lps on the hook). Take off 29Ts leaving 1B, 2C, 2D and 1C on hook, including working lp. Change to D, 1Ts through the 2C loops leaving 1B, 2C and 3D on hook.

†† *Row 27 will be the final row for the 8th petal repeat.*

Row 28: Pick up 32Ts. Take off 34Ts. Change to C, 1Ts through the 2D lps leaving 1B and 3C on hook. Cut off D leaving enough length to fasten off securely.

Row 29: Pick up 15Ts (19 lps on hook). Take off, changing to B in the last 2 lps. Cut off C leaving enough length to fasten the end securely.

Repeat from row 3 of the Background 7 times but finishing the last repeat at ††.

To Finish Last Repeat

Cont using the appropriate color to remove remaining lps. Fasten off.

Connect the two edges by picking up the upright stitch in the appropriate color.

To Complete

Place the front and back pieces together, making sure the join at the outside edge matches the other 7 points. It should be difficult to detect the join when finished. Add an edging of your choice.

Edgings

Choose from the edgings below, but please note that Edging 3 requires an additional ball of yarn.

Edging 1 Using the background color and size F/5 (4.00mm) crochet hook, work 1 row sc all around pillow. Join with sl st. Crab st back, skipping the last stitch. Fasten off and place the knot created by fastening off over the skipped st.

Edging 2 Using the background color and size F/5 (4.00mm) crochet hook, work 1 row sc all around pillow that can be divided by 6. Join with sl st. Do not turn work but cont as follows *skip 2sc, (2dc, ch2, 2dc) in next sc, skip 2sc, sl st in next sc, rep from * to end. Fasten off.

Edging 3 Using the background color and size F/5 (4.00mm) crochet hook, work 1 row sc all around pillow that can be divided by 8. Join with sl st. Do not turn work.

Row 2: *Ch1, skip 1sc, (1sc, ch1, 1hdc) in next sc, skip 1sc, (1dc, ch1, 1dc) in next sc, skip 1sc, (1hdc, ch1, 1sc) in next sc, ch1, skip 1sc, sl st in next sc, rep from * to end placing the last sl st in beg of round.

Row 3: *1sc 1hdc in next ch sp, 3dc in next ch sp, (3tr, ch1, 3tr) in next ch sp, 3dc in next ch sp, 1hdc 1sc in next ch sp, sl st on sl st, rep from * to end. Fasten off.

SIMPLE ALTERNATIVE
If you feel daunted by the patterned Tunisian pillow, try making a plain pillow back first (see below) before proceeding with the design as given above.

Plain Circle for Back of Pillow
For a neat finish it is recommended that the plain circle be worked using the background color B. Ch38.

Row 1: *Pick up 38 lps. Take off as usual.* ★★★
Row 2: *Pick up in Ts leaving the last lp unworked. Take off as usual.*
Repeat row 2 35 times.
Row 38: *Pick up 38 lps. Take off as usual.*
Rep from ★★★ 5 times, omitting row 38 on the last repeat.

Project 11: Afghan Throw

This pretty afghan throw uses puff stitches to create an attractively textured Tunisan fabric.
The throw is finished with a fringe.

Materials

9 51¾oz. (50g.) balls of Rowan DK Soft in Dusky Pink
Size H/8 (5.50mm) afghan hook
Size G/6 (4.50mm) crochet hook

Size

33 x 44in. (81 x 112cm.) before fringing

Gauge

9 sts to 2in. (5cm.); 18 rows to 4¾in. (12cm.)

Special Abbreviations

1Tpuff—Yo, insert in next st, yo and draw through lp on hook, (yo, insert in same st, yo and draw through lp on hook) twice, yo, draw through 7 lps leaving 1 lp for the st still left on the hook.

1hdc puff—This is a puff st worked into the space between the last hdc just made and the previous hdc. That is, it is worked around the stem of the last hdc and not into either the Tunisian fabric or any sts of the row beneath the hdc row.

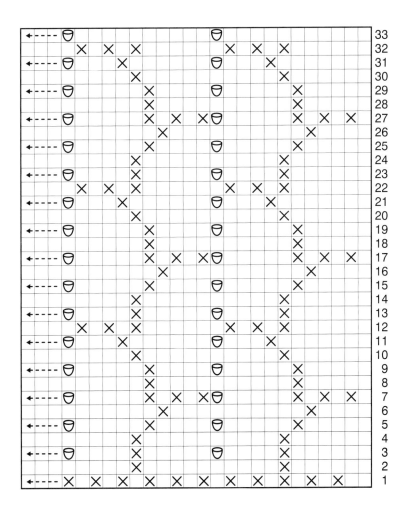

Pattern for the afghan throw

To Work

With afghan hook ch143.

Row 1: Pick up 143 lps. Take off with 1ch for lift, 1Ts, ★ch1, yo and draw through 3 lps (the working lp and 2 st lps), rep from ★ to last 2 sts, 2Ts (71 holes).

Row 2: Pick up 1Ts, ★1Ts through the 2 lps drawn together in row 1, 1Ts under 1ch of row 1, rep from ★ to last 2 sts, 2Ts (143 lps). Take off 1ch, 4Ts, ★ch2, yo and draw through 3 lps, 9Ts, rep from ★ to last 7 sts, ch2, yo and draw through 3 lps, 5Ts.

Row 3: Pick up ★4Ts, 1Ts through the 2 lps drawn tog in previous row, 1Ts in ch sp, 4Ts, 1Tpuff, rep from ★ 11 times, 4Ts, 1Ts through the 2 lps drawn tog in previous row, 1Ts in ch sp, 5Ts. Take off 1ch, 4Ts, ★ch2, yo and draw through 3 lps, 9Ts, rep from ★ to last 7 sts, ch2, yo and draw through 3 lps, 5Ts.

These 3 rows have begun the panel of eyelet holes separated by Tunisian puff stitches. Follow the graph, placing the Tunisian puff stitches in columns on alternate rows. Twelve columns of puff stitches divide the eyelet panels.

The holes are formed by the chains on the take-off row below the ones marked. This is because they do not form a hole until all the loops of the next row have been placed on the afghan hook.

Continue until work measures 33 x 44 in. (81 x 112 cm.) when smoothed from base to top.

Final row: Pick up 143 lps. Take off with 1ch for lift, 1Ts, ★ch1, yo and draw through 3 lps (the working lp and 2 sts), rep from ★ to last 2 sts, 2Ts.

With crochet hook, sl st to end inserting hook in the vertical strand of each st or ch sp to work the sl st.

Side Border

Row 1: Ch2, sc to last 2 sts, ch1, skip 1 st, 1sc, ch3, turn.

Row 2: Skip 1 st, ★1hdc puff, skip 1 st, 1hdc (do not skip a st), rep from ★ to end omitting the last ch1. Fasten off. Work the other side to correspond.

To Complete

Cut 450 pieces of yarn 10in. (25cm.) long. Make the fringe using 3 strands tog for each of the 71 holes plus the space on the sc row and the space on the hdc row (75 holes in all).

> ### SIMPLE ALTERNATIVE
> *Make a baby's blanket using sport-weight yarn, size K/10½ (7.00mm) afghan hook and size H/8 (5.50mm) crochet hook, omitting the fringe. Begin with 54 chains and patt over 5 columns of holes and 4 lines of puff stitch. Work the side borders the same. Substitute edging for fringe at top and bottom.*

CHAPTER SEVEN

Motifs And Circles Workshop

Traditional crochet has copied and then combined many of the medallion patterns found in needle and bobbin lace to make household items. Over the last 150 years these have been adapted to include fashion items also.

This chapter concentrates on making motifs and circles using fine threads and small hooks. However, one of the joys of crochet is its versatility, so if you prefer working with yarn rather than thread, try making each example in a yarn using a hook one size smaller than you would normally use with that yarn. Alternatively, if you discover that thread is definitely the medium you enjoy working with most, go back through the stitch libraries in this book and work the patterns in thread, using an appropriate hook. All of the patterns will look very different, depending on whether you make them in thread or yarn, and this will no doubt inspire you to all kinds of creative experiments.

Working With Cotton Or Linen Thread

Most crochet motifs are worked in thread rather than yarn, because crochet tends to copy lace. However, many afghans, knee rugs, and throws combine motifs worked in yarn rather than thread. This workshop and the next one concentrate on the use of steel hooks and fine cotton and linen threads, but does not exclude the use of yarn.

Points To Note

1 When working with cotton or linen thread, you normally hold the hook differently because the shape of the hook is chamfered instead of being a straight rod. Working with a shaped or tambour-style crochet hook, you must use your index finger as a stop; otherwise your stitches will be irregular in size.

2 There is no elasticity in thread, so any changes in gauge can easily be seen. Remember that in crochet the worker controls, to a great extent, the gauge of the fabric. The more relaxed you are, the looser the gauge—and vice versa.

3 Knowing which hook to use with which thread thickness is not easy for beginners, but after a little while you get the feel of the hook and thread, and know exactly what gauge you will get with a certain hook size and a particular thickness of thread. On the page opposite is a good guideline, but remember, it is only a guideline!

4 There is an enormous variety of threads suitable for fine crochet. Probably the most popular is "bedspread cotton," which is a size 10. You will encounter the term "knit-cro-sheen," which is a Coats brand of mercerized, bedspread-weight cotton with a high luster. A thicker version, "speed-cro-sheen," is a size 3. At the other end of the scale are very fine threads, sized 70, or even finer. Threads are also categorized by the number of "plies" or "cords" they contain, generally between two and eight.

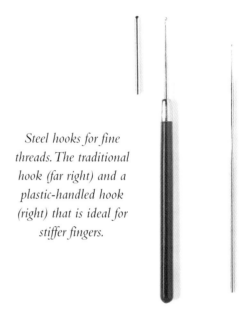

Steel hooks for fine threads. The traditional hook (far right) and a plastic-handled hook (right) that is ideal for stiffer fingers.

5 The weight or thickness of the thread can be different depending on the way it is produced. If the thread is less tight it is because there were fewer twists per inch (centimeter) during production. A traditional thread will be tightly twisted and often mercerized. The numbering of the finer threads is fairly standard throughout the world, but always check, as some manufacturers will change a numbering system as a marketing ploy.

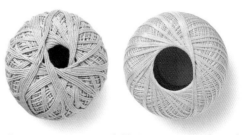

Cotton yarns are available in a variety of weights.

Weights Of Cottons

Lace weights start from around size 80 thickness up to and beyond size 100. Size 80 and 100 thread is available for crochet using a size 14 (0.60mm) hook. This is the smallest hook available, though even smaller ones can sometimes be found in antique shops, garage sales, or secondhand shops.

Traditional Weights For Heirloom Crochet

Thread weight	Suggested steel hook size
size 100	14
size 80	14
size 70	13
size 60	13
size 50	11, 12, or 13
size 40	9, 10, or 11
size 30	9 or 10
size 20	7, 8, or 9

General Weights For Making Home Accessories

Thread weight	Suggested steel hook size
size 20	6 or 7
size 10	6

General Weights For Making Fashion Items

Thread weight	Suggested hook size
size 20	4, 5, or 6 steel but also B/1
size 10	B/1 or steel 4 or 5

Thicker Weights For Heavier Household Items, Special Effects, And Fashion Crochet

Thread weight	Suggested hook size
size 8	6 steel for household, B/1 for fashion
size 5	4, 5, or 6 steel for household, C/2 for fashion
size 3	4 steel or B/1 for household, E/4, D/3, or C/2 for fashion

Starting In The Center

Many shapes can be started in the center; perhaps the most common is the much-used, often-seen "granny square" worked in scraps of leftover yarn and joined together for knee rugs and blankets. The pattern for this can be found on page 108. When starting from a central point, make sure the motif is kept flat. In order to achieve this, take note of the following points:

• The *base* of the stitch can be compressed, whereas the top or chain finish of a stitch cannot. To try to reduce the top of the stitch is impossible without reducing the whole stitch and would result in a cup shape.

• It is the *top,* not the *base,* of the stitch that determines the circumference of the circle. Therefore, when checking if a motif starting in the center is lying flat, look at the outer edge.

• The number of increases per round will depend upon the height of the stitch. A round is a row worked until it meets itself. For example, single crochet will require only 6 increases per round, whereas a triple needs 24.

• To get a perfect circle, avoid increasing in the same place on every round. When increases are placed on top of each other, they create angular shapes where the increases are, with straight rows lying between them. To avoid this, stagger where you put the increases, choosing a different place from that in the row below.

• A circle can be changed into a triangle, square, hexagon, or octagon by varying the points of increase on each round.

• When you change your stitch height because of a pattern design, you need also to change the number of increases according to the table opposite.

• To see exactly where a round starts, place a piece of contrasting thread or a safety pin at the place where the previous round has been joined.

• Should you be dissatisfied with the look of your join, do not use a slip stitch, but try this method: Remove your hook from the loop and insert it into the stitch (the hook can be inserted front to back or back to front); collect the yarn and connect the round by looping, rather than with a slip stitch. Look carefully and choose the join that is the neatest for the motif you are making.

• Ideally, work a round, then join with a slip stitch, make the necessary number of chains to lift the hook, and turn your work. By going backward and forward as though working in straight rows, you will keep the join moving outward in a straight line, rather than travelling to the left—a so-called "walking seam"—which tends to happen when working in rounds. It also happens in tubular crochet, which is worked in rounds from a foundation chain without increasing.

These two examples of tubular crochet show the direction of a "walking seam" (left) and a straight seam (right).

How To Make Flat Circles

The following table provides a set of guideline instructions for crocheting circles that lie flat. No matter how large your circle grows, the number of increases per round remains the same—there will be the same number of increases for round 50 as for round 1.

Process	single crochet	half double	double	triple
Start with:	4ch	4ch	4ch	5ch
Join with:	sl st	sl st	sl st	sl st
Chain:	1	2	3	4
Place stitches in the center of ring:	5sc	7hdc	11dc	23tr
Join with:	sl st	sl st	sl st	sl st
Turn/lift with:	ch1	ch2	ch3	ch4
Turn, place 1 st in same place as start of turning chain, then:	2sc in each st	2hdc in each st	2dc in each st	2tr in each st
This produces an increase per round of:	6sc	8hdc	12dc	24tr
Continue to increase on each:	6sc	8hdc	12dc	24tr

How To Make A Flat Triangle

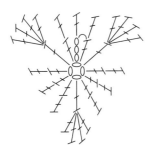

Divide the number of increases per round and place them in three places only. For single crochet that means two additional stitches, making three single crochets in one stitch. For triple that would mean as many as eight more stitches in three places or nine triples in the same place.

How To Make A Flat Square

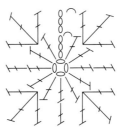

A square requires the increases to be divided by four; in single crochet that means increasing on every other round.

COMMON PROBLEMS AND
HOW TO SOLVE THEM
When making circles and semicircles watch out for the following:

Problem: *The circle has become bowl shaped.*
Action: *Check that*
• *the stitches are not being accidentally lengthened at the insertion point.*
• *the stitches are not too tight, resulting in the circle being pulled in.*
• *there are enough increases per round.*

Problem: *It is extremely difficult to keep a straight edge along the line of the diameter of a semicircle. This is due to the way the stitches lie; without the opposite semicircle, there is no opposing pull to make the stitches conform.*
Action: *The only solution is to make a segment of a circle that is fractionally less than a half.*

Problem: *If the circle is rippling instead of lying flat, there are too many stitches for the size of the circumference (remember, it is the top of the stitch that is critical in measuring circles).*
Action: *There are four possible ways to correct the problem of rippling:*
• *have fewer increases per round.*
• *use a larger crochet hook for the pattern.*
• *elongate the stitches so that the circumference is farther away from the center of the circle.*
• *check that there are no accidental increases added in a round.*

Problem: *The central section of the circle often buckles when the pattern changes from a dense or close fabric to a more lacy pattern.*
Action: *Check that the chains in the lacy section are neither too tight (which causes buckling) nor too loose (rippling). If necessary, change your hook when changing the style of stitch being crocheted.*

Joining Motifs Together

Many people are deterred from designs using motifs because of having to sew them together. An alternative to sewing motifs together is to join them with crochet.

When placing smaller circular motifs together, it is possible to join them to their neighbor when you work the last row. However, this is satisfactory only if the circles lie within the depressions made by a previous row of circles (see below left). If you want to place motifs one on top of another in columns and also in rows, it is usually necessary to add a filler (see below right). The simplest filler is a ring of six chains with one round of single crochet. The

number of singles placed in the ring should be the number of joins you need to make. From each single make enough chains to reach to the motif when slightly stretched, then join with a slip stitch and make the same number of chains to return to the ring. Join with a slip stitch and repeat until all the link chains have been worked. The number of link chains will depend upon the size of the space left between the rows and columns of motifs.

Motifs with straight edges, such as triangles and squares, can be joined together on the last round or on the right side with crab stitch to give a design line. Working single crochet on the wrong side gives a very neat join with movement and works well if there is a right and a wrong side. Alternatively the motifs could be overcast together with a large-eyed tapestry/sewing needle.

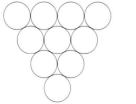 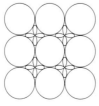

Two different ways to join motif circles together

Stitch Library

Many of the motif patterns given in this stitch library can be used to decorate fashion and household articles as an appliqué embellishment.

Lace Triangle

Ch5 and join into a ring with sl st.

Rnd 1: Ch1, 11sc into center of ring, sl st to starting ch.

Rnd 2: Ch10, skip 2sc, ★1dc, ch3, skip 1sc, 1dc, ch7, skip 1sc, rep from ★ once, 1dc, ch3, skip last sc, sl st to 3rd of 10ch.

Rnd 3: Ch3, (3dc, ch7, 4dc) in 7ch sp,★ 3dc in next 3ch sp, (4dc, ch7, 4dc) in next 7ch sp, rep from ★ once, 3dc in last 3ch sp, sl st to top of 3ch.

Rnd 4: Ch6, ★(4dc, ch5, 4dc) in next 7ch sp, ch3, skip 2dc, 1dc in next st, ch3, skip 2dc, 1sc in next dc, ch3, ★★skip 2dc, 1dc, ch3, rep from ★ once and from ★ to ★★ again, sl st to 3rd of 6ch. Fasten off.

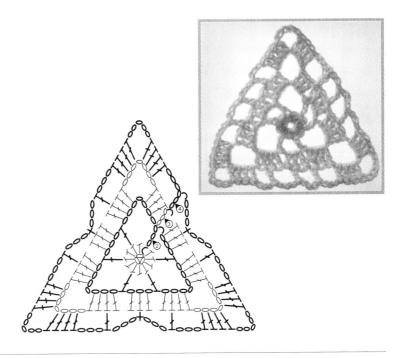

Pulsar Motif

This is a traditional open lace circle. Ch8, join with sl st.

Rnd 1: Ch8, sl st into 6th ch from hook, ★4dc into center of ring, 1p made of 5ch connected to last dc, rep from ★ 6 times, 3dc in center of ring, sl st to 3rd of 8ch at beg of round (8 p).

Rnd 2: Sl st in each of next 2ch, ch3, (1dc, ch2, 2dc) in same p, ★ch4, (2dc, ch2, 2dc) in next p, rep from ★ 6 times, ch4, sl st to top of 3ch.

Rnd 3: Sl st to next dc and next ch sp, ch3, (1dc, ch2, 2dc) into same sp, ★ch6, skip 4ch, (2dc ch2, 2dc) in next sp, rep from ★ 6 times, ch6, skip 4ch, sl st to top of 3ch.

Rnd 4: Sl st in next dc and next ch sp, ch3, (1dc, ch2, 2dc) in same sp, ★ch8, skip 6ch, (2dc, ch2, 2dc) in next sp, rep from ★ 6 times, ch8, skip 6ch, sl st to top of 3ch.

This motif can increase in size by adding another 2ch for each loop. Be cautious how big you make it, or the loops can become ungainly.

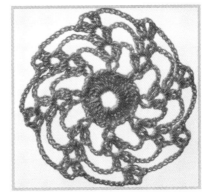

Little Gem

This motif is useful on its own, appliquéd as an embellishment, or joined together with many motifs. You will need 3 colors, A, B, and C.

Ch5 with A, join into a ring with sl st.

Rnd 1: Ch4, 2dc into 4th ch from hook, ★ch3, 1tr in ring, 2dc into base of stem of tr just made, rep from ★4 times, ch3, sl st to top of 4ch.

Rnd 2: Ch3, dc2tog over next 2dc, ★ch6, skip 3ch, dc3tog over next 3 sts, rep from ★5 times omitting last dc3tog and ending with sl st to top of first cluster. Fasten off.

Rnd 3: With B join to center of 3ch sp of first rnd, trap the 6ch of the 2nd rnd when working this rnd, ch1, 1sc into same place as 1ch, ★ch5, 1dc into top of next cluster, ch5, 1sc into 3ch arch of first rnd, rep from ★ 5 times omitting last sc and ending with sl st into first sc. Fasten off.

Rnd 4: With C join in same place, ch1, 1sc into same place as 1ch, ★ch5, skip 5ch, 3sc into next dc, ch5, skip 5ch, 1sc into next sc, rep from ★ 5 times omitting last sc and ending with sl st in first sc. Fasten off.

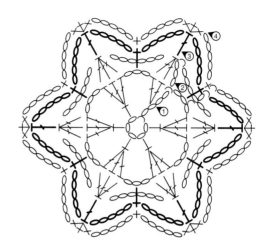

Water Wheel

Ch4, join into a ring with sl st.

Rnd 1: Ch3, 1dc in ring, ★ch2 2dc into ring, rep from ★ 5 times, ch2, sl st to top of starting ch.

Rnd 2: Ch3, 2dc in same place, 1dc, ★ch3, skip 2ch, 3dc in next dc, 1dc, rep from ★ 4 times, ch3, skip 2ch, sl st to top of 3ch [6ch lps], for hexagon sides.

Rnd 3: Ch3, 2dc in same place, 1dc, dc2tog over next 2 sts, ★ch4, skip 3ch, 3dc in next dc, 1dc, dc2tog, rep from ★ 4 times, ch4, skip 3ch, sl st to top of starting ch.

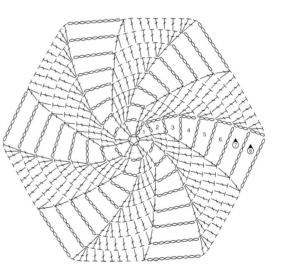

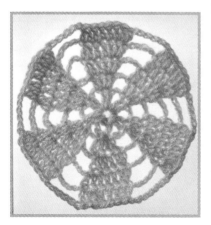

Rnd 4: Ch3, 2dc in same place, 2dc, dc2tog over next 2 sts, ★ch5, skip 4ch, 3dc in next dc, 2dc, dc2tog, rep from ★ 4 times, ch5, skip 4ch, sl st to top of starting ch.

Rnd 5: Ch3, 2dc in same place, 3dc, dc2tog over next 2 sts, ★ch6, skip 5ch, 3dc in next dc, 3dc, dc2tog, rep from ★ 4 times, ch6, skip 5ch, sl st to top of starting ch.

Rnds 6 and onward are as rnd 5 but adding an additional dc in the blocks and an additional ch in the spaces. Fasten off.

Colorful Hexagon

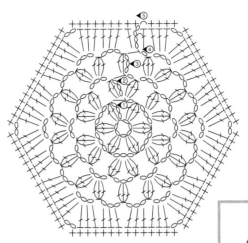

This motif can have a different color on each round or be worked in just two colors. Ch5 and join into a ring with sl st.

Rnd 1: Ch3, 2dc in center of ring, ch1, ★3dc, ch1, rep from ★ 4 times, join to top of 3ch with sl st. Fasten off.

Rnd 2: Join new color to any 1ch sp, ch3, 2dc in same sp, ch3, ★3dc in next ch sp, ch3, rep from ★ to end, join with sl st to top of 3ch. Fasten off.

Rnd 3: Join first (or new color) into any 3ch sp, ch3, (2dc, ch1, 3dc) in same ch sp, ch1, ★(3dc, ch1, 3dc) in next ch sp, ch1, rep from ★ to end, join with sl st to top of 3ch. Fasten off.

Rnd 4: Join in selected color to any 1ch sp, ch1, 1sc in every dc and every ch sp to end, join with sl st. Fasten off.

Square Of Petals

Special abbreviation: trcl—Work first tr until 2 lps rem, yo twice, insert hook into st, yo, draw through (4 lps on hook), (yo and draw through 2 lps) twice, yo twice, insert into st, yo, draw through (5 lps on hook), (yo and draw through 2 lps) twice (3 lps on hook), yo, draw through all 3 lps. Ch12, join into a ring with sl st.

Rnd 1: Ch1, 31sc into center of ring, join with sl st.

Rnd 2: Ch4, skip 3sc, ★(1dc, ch4, 1dc, ch3) in next st, skip 3sc, 1hdc, ch3, skip 3sc, rep from ★ 3 times omitting the last 1hdc, ch3, skip 3sc, sl st to 3rd of 4th ch at beg of rnd.

Rnd 3: Ch4, ★(4dc, ch3, 4dc) in 4ch sp, ch2, 1sc in hdc, ch2, rep from ★ 3 times omitting the last 2ch, 1sc, ch2, sl st to 2nd of 4ch at beg of rnd.

Rnd 4: Ch6, (1dtr, ch4, 1dtr) in same place as starting ch, ★ch3, 2trcl placing first tr in same place and 2nd tr in next 3ch sp, ch3, (1dtr, ch4, 1dtr) in same place as last tr, rep from ★ 6 times, ch3, 2trcl as before, 1tr, sl st to 3rd of 6ch, remaining 3ch count as first 3ch sp on next rnd.

Rnd 5: ★(1sc, 1hdc, 2dc) in 3ch sp, (3dc, ch3, 3dc) in 4ch sp, (2dc, 1hdc, 1sc) in 3ch sp, sl st in trcl, (1sc, 1hdc, 3dc) in 3ch sp, (2dc, 2tr, ch3, 2tr, 2dc) in 4ch sp, (3dc, 1hdc, 1sc) in 3ch sp, sl st in trcl, rep from ★ 7 times. Fasten off.

Flemish Motif

Special abbreviation: scl—Insert hook into lp, yo, draw through to front, insert hook into next lp, yo, bring to front, yo, draw through all 3 lps on hook. Ch8, join into a ring with sl st.

Rnd 1: Ch1, 16sc into ring, sl st to first sc (16 sts).

Rnd 2: Ch12 (to count as 1tr and ch8), skip first 2sc, ★1tr into next sc, ch8, skip 1sc, rep from ★ 6 times, sl st to 4th of 12ch.

Rnd 3: Ch1, ★(1s,c 1hdc, 1dc, 3tr, ch4 [for a p by inserting hook through top of tr just made and working sl st to close], (2tr, 1dc, 1hdc, 1scl) all into next 8ch arch, work rep from ★ 6 more times, sl st to first sc. Fasten off.

Petite Flower

This is an ideal filler stitch.
Ch8, join into a ring with sl st.

Rnd 1: Ch4, 2trcl [see page 107] into center of ring, ★ch6, 3trcl in center of ring, rep from ★ 6 times, ch6, join to top of first cluster with 1sl st. 3trcl in centre of ring.

Rnd 2: Sl st into 6ch sp, ★(1sc 1p 1sc in 6ch sp) 3 times, 1sc 1p in same sp, 1sc in next sp, rep from ★ 7 times omitting the last 1p 1sc, sl st to beg of rnd.

Granny Square

Try this traditional square. Ch4 with M, join into a ring with sl st.

Rnd 1: Ch3, 2dc into ring ★ch1, 3dc, rep from ★ twice, ch1, join to 3rd of 4ch at beg of row with sl st. Break off yarn.

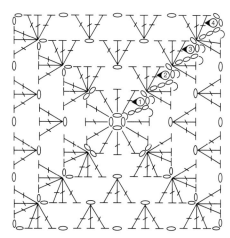

Rnd 2: Attach C to any ch sp, (ch3, 2dc, ch1, 3dc, ch1) in that sp, ★(3dc, ch1, 3dc, ch1) in next sp, rep from ★ twice, join to 3rd of 3ch with sl st. Break off yarn.

Rnd 3: Attach M to any side sp, i.e. any sp bet groups (or blocks), ch3, 2dc, ch1, ★3dc, ch1, 3dc in next sp, (ch1, 3dc) in next sp, ch1, rep from ★ twice, (ch1, 3dc) in next sp, ch1, join with sl st. Break off yarn.

Project 12: Hats And Bags

These lightweight hats and bags are perfect for summer weather and make full use of the shaping skills you have learned in this workshop. Try working the child's variations for quicker projects.

Hats

Materials

Bedspread-weight (size 10) mercerized cotton thread, approx. 575yd. (530m.) in either grey or pale pink for each hat
Size B/1 (2.50mm) hook

Size

To fit average head

Gauge

12dc and 6 rows to 2in. (5cm.)

Adult's Hat

Work with two balls together at all times. There should be no difficulty in working the two balls as one yarn, so you will not need to twist the two threads together. The work is turned on each round.

To Work

Ch3, ensuring that the slip knot slides closed from the tail end.
Rnd 1: Into the top lp of the first ch (i.e. the slip knot) place 11dc, tighten the slip knot and secure after working one or two rnds; sl st into 3rd ch to join, ch3, turn (12 sts).
Rnd 2: 1dc in same place as turning ch, ★2dc in next st, rep from ★ to end, sl st to top of turning ch, ch3, turn (24 sts).
Rnd 3: ★2dc in next st, 1dc, rep from ★ to last st, 2dc in last st, join with sl st to top of turning ch, ch3, turn (36 sts).
Rnd 4: 1dc in same place as turning ch, 2dc, ★2dc in next st, 2dc, rep from ★ to end, join with sl st to top of turning ch, ch5, turn (48 sts).
Rnd 5: ★2dtr in next st, 1dtr, rep from ★ to end, join with sl st to top of turning ch, ch3, turn (96 sts).

Rnd 6: 3dc, ★2dc in next st, 6dc, rep from ★ to last 2 sts, 2dc, join with sl st to top of turning ch, ch3, turn (108 sts). Work 4 more rnds inc 12 sts evenly to form a circle (156 sts).
Rnd 11: Ch2 to make 5ch, 1dtr in each st to end, ch3, turn (156 sts).
Rnd 12: 1dc in same place as turning ch, ★35dc, 2dc in next st, rep from ★ twice, 35dc, join with sl st to top of turning ch, ch3, turn (160 sts).
Work 3 more rnds in dc, 1 rnd dtr, and 2 rnds in dc without increasing.
Rnd 19: 1dc in same place as turning ch, ★36dc, 2dc in next st, rep from ★ twice, 36dc, join with sl st to top of turning ch, ch3, turn (164 sts).
Rnd 20: 1dc in same place as turning ch, ★37dc, 2dc in next st, rep from ★ twice, 37dc, join with sl st to top of turning ch, ch3, turn (168 sts).
Rnd 21: 1dc in same place as turning ch, ★38dc, 2dc in next st, rep from ★ twice, 38dc, join with sl st to top of turning ch, ch3, turn (172 sts).
Rnd 22: 1dc in same place as turning ch, ★39dc, 2dc in next st, rep from ★ twice, 39dc, join with sl st to top of turning ch, ch3, turn (176 sts).
Work another 5 rnds in dc without shaping. Fasten off. Securely sew in the ends.

Child's Hat

Work as for adult's hat to end of rnd 6.
Work 1 more rnd increasing 12 sts evenly to form a circle (120 sts).
Rnd 8: In dc without increasing.
Rnd 9: Ch2 to make 5ch, 1dtr in each st to end, ch3, turn (120 sts).
Rnd 10: Work in dc without increasing.
Rnd 11: 1dc in same place as turning ch, ★29dc, 2dc in next st, rep from ★ twice, 29dc, join with sl st to top of turning ch, ch3, turn (124 sts).
Rnd 12: 1dc in same place as turning ch, ★30dc, 2dc in next st, rep from ★ twice, 30dc, join with sl st to top of turning ch, ch3, turn (128 sts).

Rnd 13: 1dc in same place as turning ch, ★31dc, 2dc in next st, rep from ★ twice, 31dc, join with sl st to top of turning ch, ch3, turn (132 sts).

Rnd 14: 1dc in same place as turning ch, ★32dc, 2dc in next st, rep from ★ twice, 32dc, join with sl st to top of turning ch, ch3, turn (136 sts).

Work another 8 rows in dc without shaping. Fasten off. Securely sew in ends.

Bags

Materials

Bedspread-weight (size 10) mercerized cotton thread, approx. 1,730yd. (1,590m.) in burgundy for the adult's bag and/or approx. 1,150yd. (1,060m.) in bright pink for the child's bag
2½yd. (2.5m.) of rope or washing line for the adult's bag and/or 1yd. (1 m.) of the same for the child's bag
Size B/1 (2.50mm) hook

Size

Adult's: 10in. (25cm.) diameter; 12in. (30cm.) deep
Child's: 5in. (12.5cm.) diameter; 6¹/2in. (16.5cm.) deep

Gauge

12dc and 6 rows to 2in. (5cm.)

Adult's Bag

As with the adult's and child's hats, work with two balls together at all times. There should be no difficulty in working the two balls as one yarn, so you will not need to twist the two threads together. The work is not turned on each round.

To Work

Ch3, ensuring that the slip knot slides closed from the tail end.

Rnd 1: Into the top lp of the first ch (i.e. the slip knot) place 10dc, tighten the slip knot and secure after working one or two rnds; sl st into 3rd ch to join, ch2, do not turn (11 sts).

Rnd 2: ★2dc in sp bet dc, rep from ★ to end, join with

sl st to top of turning ch (21 sts).

Inc by 10 sts on each rnd until 17 rnds have been completed (171 sts).

Next rnd: sc to end, ch1, turn.

Work 1 rnd sc ending with ch2, turn.

† Work 9 rnds of dc bet dc without shaping, finishing last rnd with ch1.

Work 2 rnds sc.

Rep from † twice.

Work 1 rnd of dc bet dc, then 4 rnds dec 4 sts on each rnd (139 sts).

Work 2 rnds sc. Fasten off.

Handles

Ch8.

Row 1: 1sc in 3rd ch from hook, 1sc in each ch to end, ch1, turn (6 sts).

Row 2: sc to end, ch1, turn.

Rep rnd 2 130 times.

Cut rope in half and double. Enclose rope in crocheted strip leaving 4–6 rows free. Either sew or sc the edges together, inserting the rope as you join. Securely attach the flat ends to the bag. Repeat to make a second handle.

Child's Bag

Work as for Adult's bag until 9 rnds have been completed (91 sts).

† Work 5 rnds of dc bet dc without shaping, finishing the last rnd with ch1.

Next rnd: 1sc in each stitch to end, ch1, turn.

Work 1 rnd sc ending with ch2, turn.

Rep from † twice.

Work 1 rnd of dc bet dc and a further 4 rnds dec 4 sts on each rnd (71 sts).

Work 2 rnds sc ending with ch2, turn. Fasten off.

Handles

Ch13.

Row 1: 1sc in 3rd ch from hook, 1sc in each ch to end, ch1, turn (12 sts).

Rnd 2: sc to end, ch1, turn.

Rep row 2 60 times.

Cut rope in half and fold into four. Complete as for the adult's bag.

Project 13: Motif Pillow

This decorative pillow is made from 16 three-color motifs which are worked together in rows as you crochet. Be adventurous and vary the colors of the motifs to match your own furnishings.

Materials

Sport-weight cotton yarn, approx. 225yd. (210m.) for the back of pillow
Approx. 75yd. (70m.) of the same in each of white, lilac, oyster, pink, bright green, dark green, turquoise, pale blue, dark blue, orange, and red
Size F/5 and 7 (4.00mm and 4.50mm) hooks
Pillow form 18in. (45cm.) square

Size

16in. (40cm.) square

Gauge

Each motif is 4in. (10cm.) square.

Special Abbreviations

A = Central color of motif
B = Middle color of motif
C = Outer color of motif

To Work

For a good fit, make the front before the back. Carefully follow the pattern to work the different motifs in the correct sequence.

First Motif (corner motif)

With the larger hook and A ch5, join into a ring with sl st.
Rnd 1: Ch4, (1hdc, ch2) 7 times, join to 2nd of 4ch with sl st. Fasten off.
Rnd 2: Join B to any 2ch sp, ch3, dc3tog in same sp, *ch4, dc4tog in next sp, rep from * to end, ch4, join to top of 3ch, fasten off.
Rnd 3: Join in C to top of any cluster, ch1, 1sc in sp,

*ch2, 1dc in hdc of rnd 1 enclosing 4ch lp of rnd 2, ch2, 1sc in top of next cluster, rep from * all around omitting sc at end, join to first sc with sl st.
Rnd 4: Sl st into next ch sp, ch1, 1sc in same sp, ch3, *1sc in next sp, ch3, rep from * to end joining with sl st to first sc.
Rnd 5: Sl st into next ch sp, (ch3, 1dc, ch2, 2dc) all in same space, *ch2, (1sc in next sp, ch3) twice, (ch2, 2dc, ch2, 2dc) in next sp, †† rep from * twice more, ch2, (1sc in next sp, ch3) twice, ch2, join with sl st to top of 3ch, Fasten off.

Second Motif (links to another motif on one side)

Work rnds 1–4 as first motif.
Rnd 5: Sl st into next ch sp, (ch3, 1dc, ch1, sl st) into corner 2ch sp of first motif. *Make sure WS of both motifs are tog and cont working from the front.* Ch1, 2dc in same sp of second motif, ch2, (1sc in next sp, ch1, sl st in corresponding sp of first motif, ch1) twice, ch2, 2dc, ch1, sl st in next corner of first motif, ch1, 2dc in same sp of second motif, continue as rnd 5 of first motif from ††.
Rep the second motif twice to form base row of the pillow.
Work the second motif once but connect it to the first motif of the base row to begin the next row of 4 motifs.

Third Motif (links to other motif on two sides)

Work rnds 1-4 as first motif.
Rnd 5: Sl st into next ch sp, (ch3, 1dc, ch1, sl st) into corner 2ch sp of previous motif, ch1, 2dc in same sp or present motif, {ch2, (1sc in next sp, ch1, sl st in corresponding sp of previous motif, ch1) twice, ch2} 2dc, ch1, sl st in next corner of previous motif which also includes the corner sp of the motif on the row below, ch1, 2dc in same sp of present motif, work from { to } once, 2dc, ch1, sl st in next corner of previous motif, ch1, 2dc in same sp of present motif, continue as rnd 5 of first motif from ††.
Rep from ### twice to give 4 rows of 4 motifs.

Small Motif (decorative motif)

With the smaller hook, ch3, making sure the slip knot can slide from the short end and not the ball end.

Row 1: 5sc in top lp of first ch made.

Row 2: ★(1sc, ch1, 1dc, ch1, 1sc) in next st, rep from ★ 4 times, join to first sc with sl st. Fasten off. Tighten the center from the slip knot end and fasten end in.

Make another 8 motifs in a variety of colors. Attach the small motifs to the front of the pillow where 4 motifs join.

Back Of Pillow

The back should be ¾–1½in. (2–4cm.) less than the front of the pillow.

Note: check the number of stitches you have after working 3 or 4 rows. If there are too few stitches, calculate how many extra stitches you need, and start again with additional chains. If you have too many stitches, calculate how many stitches need to be removed and start again with fewer chains.

With the larger hook ch65.

Row 1: 1sc in 3rd ch from hook, sc to end, ch3, turn (64 sts).

Row 2: dc to end, ch1, turn.

Row 3: sc to end, ch3, turn.

Rep rows 2 and 3 until length of front has been reached, ending on a sc row.

To Complete

Darn in all the loose ends of yarn.

Sew the front to the back, remembering to insert the pillow form before completing the fourth side.

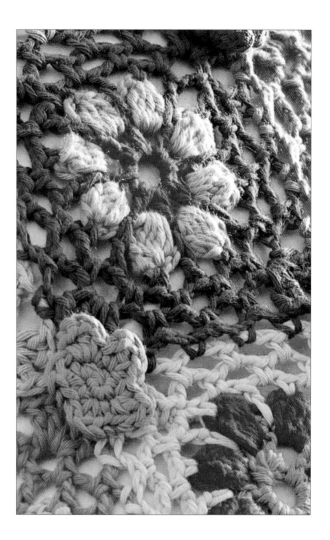

SIMPLE ALTERNATIVES
• *Both the large motif and the small motif can be used as an embellishment. Make a selection of them and attach them to a plain pillow cover in a random pattern. You can vary the large motif by stopping after round 3.*
• *Work an additional round of sc with picots on the large motif. Make two of these and sew them together to make a lavender bag.*

Project 14: Floral Decorations

Use the skills you have learned in this workshop to create a beautiful selection of crochet flowers to use as embellishments for clothes and accessories. Try varying the weight of yarn and size of hook to make flowers in a wide range of sizes.

Violet

Materials

Small amounts of size 10 crochet cotton in pale purple, dark purple, and yellow
Size 7 steel(1.50mm) hook

Size

1in. (2.5cm.) wide

To Make

Using dark purple, ch5 and join with sl st into ring, ★ into the ring work ch4, 3dtr, ch4, 1sc, rep from ★4 times (5 petals worked). Fasten off.

Optional

Work another 9 violets, making some in the pale purple and some with 2 or 3 petals in the paler shade and the remainder in the dark purple. Using green thread, cover a padded hairband with hdc by making a chain longer than the hairband and working a sufficient number of rows to cover the top. Sew to the underside. Tuck in the ends and sew on the violets.

Sunflower

Materials

Small amounts size 10 crochet cotton in yellow and brown
Size 4 steel (2.00mm) hook

Size

Large flower: 3¼in. (8cm.) wide
Medium flower: 2¾in. (7cm.) wide

Large Flower

Use 2 strands of thread together throughout. With brown
ch 2.
Rnd 1: (RS) 6sc in 2nd ch from hook, sl st to join, ch1,
turn (6sc).
Rnd 2: 1sc in same place, ★2sc in next sc, rep from ★ to
end, sl st to join, ch1, turn (12sc).
Rnd 3: sc to end (12sc). Fasten off leaving long end
for sewing.
Join in yellow for petals to any sc with RS facing, ★ch10,
sl st into 3rd ch from hook, 1sc, 1hdc, 3dc, 1hdc, 1sc, sl st
in next brown st, rep from ★ 11 times, sl st to first of 8ch
(12 petals).
Fasten off, leaving long end for sewing.

Smaller Flower

Use two strands of thread together throughout. With
brown ch5, join together with sl st.
Rnd 1: (RS) 7sc in ring, sl st to join. Finish off, leaving
long end for sewing.
Join in yellow for petals to any sc with RS facing,
★ch10, sl st into 3rd ch from hook, 1sc, 1hdc, 3dc, 1hdc,
1sc, sl st in next brown st, rep from ★ 7 times, sl st to
first of 8ch (8 petals).
Fasten off, leaving long end for sewing.

To Complete

Fasten off all ends.

Pansy

Materials

Small amounts of size 10 crochet cotton in magenta
and black
Size 7 steel (1.50mm) hook

Size

From edge of large petal to edge of medium petal:
8¾in. (3.5cm.)

To Work

Using black thread, ch9, join into ring with sl st.
Rnd 1: Ch3, 2sc in ring (ch7, 3sc in ring) 4 times, ch7,
sl st in top of 3ch at beg of rnd. Change to magenta.
Rnd 2: Ch3, (skip 1sc, 1sc, 15dc in next space, 1sc) twice,
rep instructions between parentheses, ★ skip 1sc, ch1, put
everything in brackets in next ch sp, [(1dc, ch1) twice,
(1tr, ch1) 3 times, (1dtr ch1) 5 times, (1tr, ch1) 3 times
(1dc, ch1) twice], 1sc, ch1, rep from ★ until another large
petal is completed, join with sl st.
Fasten off.

To Complete

Sew in the loose ends of yarn.

SIMPLE ALTERNATIVES
• *For smaller flower use size 20 cotton and a
size 9 steel (1.25mm) crochet hook.*
• *To make larger flowers, try size 3 cotton and a
size B/1 (2.50mm) crochet hook.*

CHAPTER EIGHT

Filet Crochet Workshop

CROCHET BEGAN AS an imitation of the various kinds of bobbin and needle laces, using fine cotton and an appropriate size of tambour embroidery hook. Looking at old patterns, you will see that many words used to describe different kinds of crochet are the same as those used for types of lace; you will even come across "crochet tatting"—referring to a kind of lace made with a shuttle. "Crochet tatting" imitates the style of this work, using a hook and crochet stitches. Filet crochet, however, was the most prolific, as it copied filet lace easily and did not require a written pattern.

Any crochet that is worked in relatively fine yarn or thread and uses a stitch that produces an open fabric is often referred to as "crochet lace" or "lace crochet." Unless the pattern really does copy one of the traditional laces, however, the term is not an accurate one.

Filet Crochet

The name "filet crochet" is a term handed down from the mid-nineteenth century, when crochet began to copy the patterns of laces. Indeed, there are many patterns available dating back to the 1840s—have a look in your local museum or library. Filet lace is a very smooth lace worked with a needle. The crochet copy of filet designs produces ridges on each row, unlike the real filet lace, which has nothing to give it contrast or shadows. One reason for the popularity of filet crochet is the ease with which it can be charted on graph paper using a cross for a block and leaving the square blank for a space. This makes it relatively simple to create geometric designs and even text.

Stitches Used

Only two stitches are used in the simple squared network of filet crochet—chain and double crochet. These form either a block or a space.

Block (blk) = 3 doubles (dc) per square
Space (sp) = 2 chains 1 double (ch2, 1dc) per square

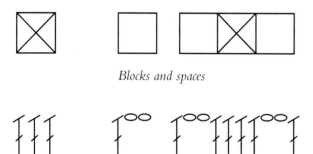

Blocks and spaces

The same blocks and spaces written in symbols

Doubles worked on top of doubles go under two strands of thread as usual. However, if the doubles are worked in a space, the first two doubles should be worked directly into the space under the chains. There will be occasions when it is prudent to work the doubles directly into each chain of a space, but this is very rare.

Bars And Lacets

The common background mesh for filet designs is a network of squares, made by working a series of spaces—that is, two chains, one double, making each double sit on top of the one in the row below.

Bars and lacets use two squares on a piece of graph paper, with the lacets looking like wings and the bar being unmarked.

A bar = ch5, 1dc (over 6 stitches, i.e. 2 squares)
A lacet = ch3, 1sc under the bar (i.e. the 5ch sp), ch3, 1dc on dc.

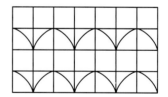

Bars and lacets

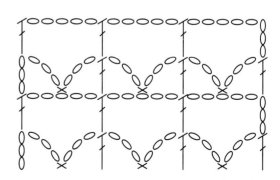

The same bars and lacets written in symbols

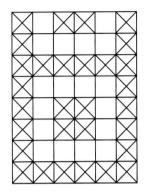

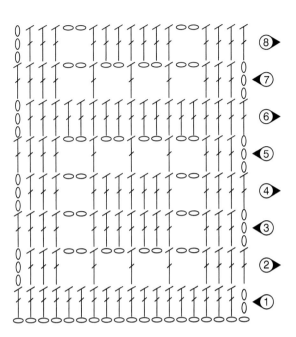

This shows the same stitch pattern drawn with both chart marking and symbols. As you can see, the pattern that is drawn with blocks and spaces takes up much less space and is easier to follow.

Calculating Chains To Start Work On A Piece Of Filet Crochet

In order to calculate the number of chains you will need in your foundation chain, follow the instructions in the chart below. As an example, the chart below shows how to calculate the number of chains required in the foundation chain for a chart with six squares.

	Example: a chart has 6 squares and starts with a block.	Example: a chart has 6 squares and starts with a space.
Multiply the number of squares in the chart by 3:	18	18
Add 1 chain for turning:	1	1
Add 2 if starting with a block:	2	2
If starting with a space add another 2:		2
Total number of chains required:	21	23

Useful Notes About Filet Crochet

Filet crochet is traditionally used for household linen, which is then placed over tables, chairs, trays, plates, etc. With either cotton or mixed fibers in a smooth yarn, you can create interesting fashion designs. However, textured yarns frequently detract from the pattern and the intended effect, so make a sample piece before working the whole filet design.

Insertion Strips

Insertion strips are crocheted strips usually placed in a piece of woven fabric. However, they can also be used to add interest to a plain crocheted fabric composed of single or double crochet, for example. An insertion strip usually has both sides worked with a very smooth and plain edge for ease of inserting (see pages 142 for various ways of incorporating crochet as an insertion).

Edgings

The difference between an insertion and an edging is that an edging usually has only one straight edge, unlike an insertion strip, which has two straight edges. Filet edgings can be castellated, scalloped, or in a Vandyke (i.e. chevron) shape.

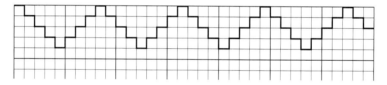

Vandyke edging

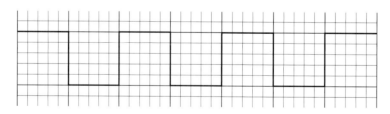

Castle edging

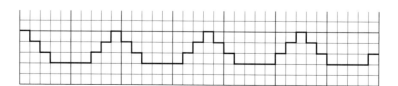

Scallop edging

Increasing And Decreasing In Filet

Unlike all other kinds of crochet, filet cannot be decreased or increased at the sides in a smooth curve. This is because increases and decreases in filet are not stitch by stitch, but square by square. Therefore, if you want a true scalloped edge, add a final row using chain and picots or some other decorative edge.

Increasing At The Beginning Of A Row

Increasing at the beginning of a row of filet is simple. Additional chains are worked at the end of the previous row. For a space, make seven chains and place one double in the last stitch of the previous row. If the increase is starting with a block, five chains are needed; work one double in the fourth chain from the hook, one double in the next chain, and then continue the crochet over the previous row as usual.

Increasing At The End Of A Row

Increasing at the end of a row in filet does, however, require some thought, particularly if you need to shape both edges symmetrically. Do this by making long stitches.

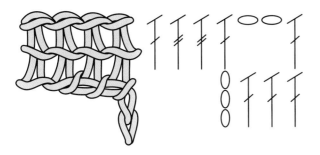

Increasing using a triple

For a block, place one triple in the same place as the last double. There has to be a double in the last stitch or the square of the filet pattern would not be complete. Now place one triple in the last crossover strand of the previous triple (see above). Place one double in the last crossover strand of the previous

triple, and you will find that the triple bends to the height of a double and gives you the equivalent of a base chain. The two triples and one double make three stitches for a block.

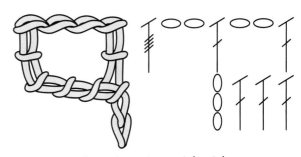

Increasing using a triple triple

For a space, make two chains and one triple triple placed in the last double of the last square. The triple triple gives enough length for the three base chains and one double (see above).

Decreasing At The Beginning Of A Row

Decreasing at the beginning of a row in filet is not difficult; simply slip-stitch to the next square and work as usual.

Decreasing At The End Of A Row

Decreasing at the end of a row in filet is equally simple. Just stop one square from the end and turn.

Stitch Library

All the patterns in this stitch library are worked using a square grid. For ease of working out, you will find that the number of chains is given for each design. The Alternating Tiles and Background Waves could be used as allover patterns—while the other designs are motifs to be worked singly or in groups.

Southern Cross

62ch, working 1dc in
8th ch from hook
= 19 squares.

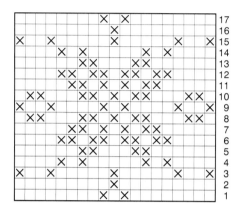
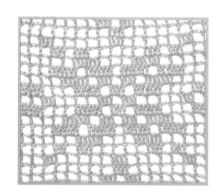

Alternating Tiles

54ch, working 1dc in
4th ch from hook
= 17 squares.

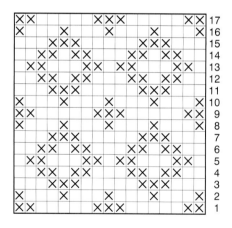
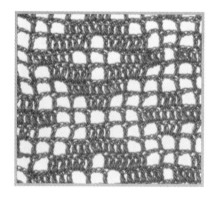

Background Waves

44ch, working 1dc in
8th ch from hook
= 13 squares.

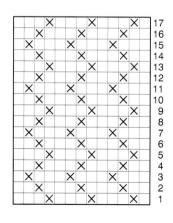

Union Flag

86ch, working
1dc in 8th ch
from hook
= 21 squares.

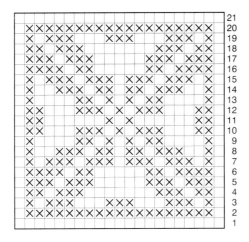

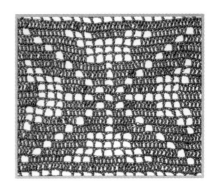

Butterfly

98ch, working
1dc in 8th ch
from hook
= 31 squares.

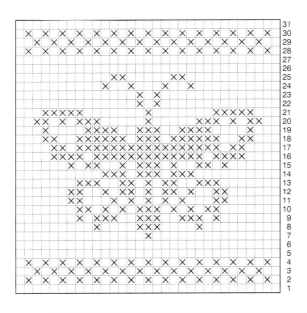

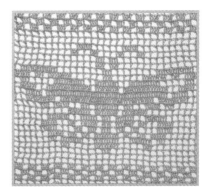

Orchid Blooms

84ch, working
1dc in 4th ch
from hook
= 27 squares.

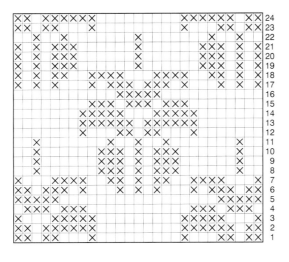

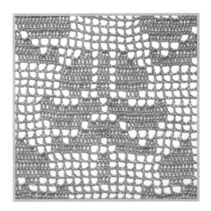

Project 15: Filet Slippers

These lacy crochet slippers are worked in lightweight cotton for a delicate finish. If you prefer, you could work the slippers in a slightly thicker yarn and line them.

Materials

Size 20 tightly spun, mercerized crochet cotton, approx. 283yd. (260m.) in blue
Size 6 steel (1.75mm) hook
Small amount of the narrowest elastic or shirring elastic (enough to stretch comfortably around the ankle)

Size

One size (average woman's foot)

Gauge

7 squares wide and 8 squares tall to 2in. (5cm.)

To Work

Ch28.
Row 1: 1dc in 4th ch from hook, dc to end, ch4, turn (26 sts).
Row 2: (1dc, ch1) in each st to end, ch5, turn (51 sts).
Row 3: (1dc, ch2) in each dc to end (76 sts)—25 squares for the filet pattern.
Follow rows 4–22 on the chart.
Row/rnd 23: Ch8 for 2-square inc, 1dc in 4th ch from hook, 2dc to make first inc square. Follow chart inc 1 square with ch2, 1trtr at end of row. Join with sl st to the turning ch at beg of row to form a tube. It is important the work be turned on every rnd for it to look the same as the first 22 rows.
Follow the chart decreasing at the symbol ∧. To dec over 2 sps, omit 2ch and work dc2tog.
To dec over a blk work dc4tog.
Sew the heel and the toe with slipstitch or other flat seam.

Edge

Rnd 1: Join the thread to the top of the first st in row 4 to the right of the heel, 1sc in top of each st to where

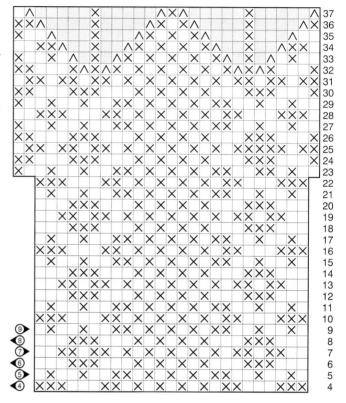

Pattern for slippers

heel has been joined, 1dc in join, 1sc in top of each st to row 4 at left of heel. ★Cont in sc placing 1sc in top of each row end, and 1sc in sp created by the dc or turning ch. ★★ 1sc in each st across top drawing base of inc tog. Work from ★ to ★★ once.
Rnd 2: Work 1sc over elastic into each st, join with sl st. Fasten off.

SIMPLE ALTERNATIVES
• *Make a smaller size by working with the same thread but using a size 7 steel (1.50mm) hook.*
• *Use a size 4 steel (2.00mm) hook for a larger slipper size.*

Project 16: Lace Shade Edging

This pretty lace panel is formed with a 42-row repeat in filet. You could adapt this pattern to edge soft furnishings or even clothing.

Materials

Size 20 tightly spun, mercerized crochet cotton, approx. 425yd. (390m.) in blue
Size 6 steel (1.75mm) hook
Shade to which the edging is attached

Size

10½in. (27cm.) deep
Each pattern repeat is 7½in. (19cm.) in length.

Gauge

10 sps to 4in. (10cm.)

To Work

The edging is worked from the short width of the design. This is to allow as many pattern repeats as necessary for the panel to fit your chosen shade. If necessary, refer to the information about increasing on page 123.
Ch81 to give 26 squares on the chart.
Row 1: 1dc in 4th ch from hook, 5dc, (ch2, 1dc) 5 times to give 5 sps, 57dc to give 19 blks, ch5, turn.
Row 2: Skip 2 sts, 1dc in dc, 18dc to give 6 blks, ch2, skip 2dc, 1dc for 1 sp, 9dc for 3 blks, ch2, skip 2dc, 1dc for 1 sp, 18dc to give 6 blks, (ch2, skip 2dc, 1dc) 7 times for 7 sps, 3dc, ch9 for a 2-square extension and turning.
Row 3: 1dc in 4th ch from hook, 6dc for 2 blks, 9 sps, 4 blks, 3 sps, 1 blk, 3 sps, 4 blks, 2 sps, ch5 to turn.
Follow the chart from here. The pattern repeat is 42 rows beginning with row 2. To complete, end with row 1. Pin to size and press, then attach the edging to the window shade.

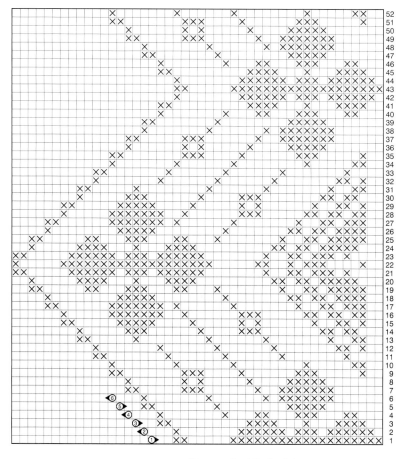

Pattern for blind edging

CHAPTER NINE

Broomstick Lace Workshop

BROOMSTICK LACE (OR JIFFY LACE) is an open fabric using less yarn than Tunisian crochet, as it is a pattern of crocheted holes. The hook size is chosen for the thickness of the yarn or thread and not for the diameter of the broomstick. It is the size of the broomstick (also called a jiffy lace needle) that determines the depth of hole and therefore the height of each row. As in Tunisian crochet, all the loops are put on in one direction and crocheted off in the other. There is also a right and wrong side to the work. My personal choice of which side to have as the right side, when using smooth yarn, is to place the curved chain on the right side. However, with a heavily textured yarn such as mohair, I tend to choose the side without the chains, as I like the cascade look the pattern gives in this yarn.

Now that you have many crochet skills, and have been able to experiment for yourself, broomstick offers another chance to "play"—try adding crab stitch to the curved chain look as a surface trim, or you could thread ribbon through the rows if you want to make the fabric look denser.

Basic Broomstick Technique

Try working broomstick lace with a size 50 (25mm) broomstick needle, worsted-weight yarn and a size H/8 (5.50mm) crochet hook. The broomstick can be held in many different ways, but I suggest placing it firmly on the chair between your legs; this lets you have both hands free and avoids twisting your body. Alternatively, put the broomstick between the arm of a chair and your thigh, or place it under one arm.

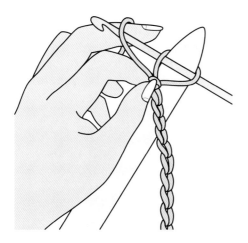

1 Make 20 loose chains. Expand the last loop and place it over the broomstick, tightening it to fit snugly.

2 ★Keeping the chain at the left-hand side of the broomstick, insert the hook into the next chain, yo, pull through to front, extend the loop and place on the broomstick. Repeat from ★ to end of chain. There should be 20 loops on the broomstick, and these are very easy to count.

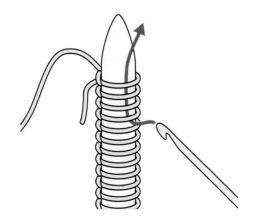

3 †Give the broomstick a half turn so that the yarn lies behind the needle. Remove the loops by inserting the hook into the first 4 loops and with the hook pointing in the same direction as the tip of the broomstick needle.

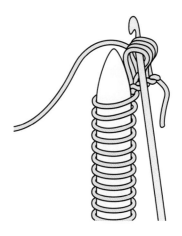

4 Yo, draw yarn through loosely, chain 1. This chain is really the slip knot and does not count as a stitch. Keep the yarn on top of the group of loops to prevent the side of the work from gathering up like a drawstring.

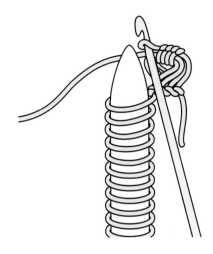

5 Into the center of this group of loops work 1 single crochet for each loop removed, in this case 4 single crochet. *Remove next 4 loops, inserting the hook as before, 4 single crochet in center of the group of loops, repeat from * to end. ††

TIP

It is easier if you place the thumb of the hand holding the broomstick into the group of loops before inserting the hook. This gives better control and a more even gauge.

---

6 Because there is already 1 loop on the hook when you remove the second and subsequent groups of loops, there is no need to make a chain as in the first group.

Give the needle another half turn. Extend the loop and place it over the broomstick, *insert hook into next stitch under 2 strands, yo, draw yarn to front and put on broomstick, rep from * to end. Remove loops again by working from † to ††. Continue picking up loops in one direction and removing them in the other, until you have the desired length.

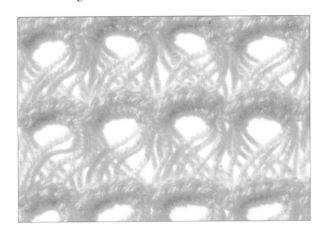

An example of basic broomstick crochet

Increasing And Decreasing

Increasing in broomstick is very easy—simply add more stitches in the group where the increase is required. Decreasing is equally easy—just put fewer stitches in the group where a decrease is required.

It will take two full pattern rows to complete either an increase or a decrease. For instance, in a pattern taking the loops off in groups of four, two single crochet (not four single) are worked in the four loops for a decrease. On the next row there will be a shortage of two loops. These two loops should be added to the last group of four loops. Place four single crochet into these, completing a decrease of one full group. Odd numbers can be decreased in a similar way by first placing two single crochet in a group of five loops and then on the

next row using the full five single crochet once more in the group of five loops, plus the two loops.

Increasing a group of four loops is worked in reverse. Put six single crochet in the group of four loops, but on the next row when there are six loops, work four single crochet in four loops and four single crochet in two loops. Odd numbers can be increased in a similar way, first placing three single crochet in a group of five loops and then on the next row using the full five single crochet once more in the three loops.

Joining Yarn In Broomstick

You may put it down to the thrift instilled in me as a young girl, but in broomstick lace, I prefer to join in a new ball of yarn whenever necessary, even if it is in the middle of a row. This is not only because it is a thrifty technique, but also because it is often rather difficult to assess just how much yarn you will need to complete a row. Imagine putting 300 loops onto the broomstick, only for the yarn to run out with another 25 loops to make. Sewing the yarn ends together is a crafty way to avoid this potential problem.

Ways Of Joining Yarn

It is generally easier to join yarn at the beginning of a row. However, when vast numbers of stitches are being used, this may be uneconomical, due to the length of drop in each loop.

If you need to join yarn while working single crochet into the groups, use the normal way of joining yarn into a fabric of basic crochet stitches. However, you may need to join yarn while placing the loops on the broomstick, and with the following method the join is difficult to detect.

Thread the end of the yarn from the new ball into a sewing or tapestry needle. Stretch the end of the old yarn over the fingers and sew the new yarn through the old yarn, using running stitches, as shown for at least 3in. (7cm.). Remove the tapestry needle from the new yarn, and pull the two ends gently until they become tight and are approximately the same thickness as the original thread. Be careful not to pull too hard, or you will have to do it all over again! If any ugly ends of yarn stick out of the join, snip them closely with a sharp pair of scissors. Once you have done this you can continue the work as if you were using one continuous thread.

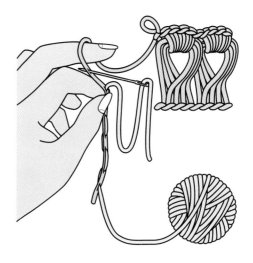

Sewing the new ball of yarn to the end of the old one

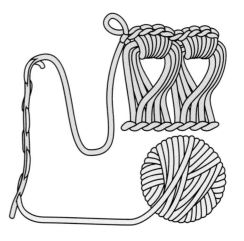

Having pulled the two ends of yarn gently to achieve the same thickness, you are now ready to trim the ends

Joining Seams In Broomstick

Crochet should have seams that are not easily visible to the eye. There are three different ways that you can join pieces of crocheted broomstick lace: side to side, chain to chain, or curved top to curved top. Depending on how you want to join the sections together, choose one of the methods below.

Joining The Sides Of The Rows

There are two excellent ways of joining the sides of the broomstick rows.

With a tapestry needle Thread some matching yarn into a tapestry needle, and attach to the start of the seam. ★Work three or four overcasting stitches into the single crochet or starting chain. Carry the yarn loosely behind the open pattern to the next row of single crochet. This loose thread does not show, as it fits into the strands of the broomstick crochet as part of the pattern. Be careful to make it long enough to lie without pulling from one single crochet row to the next. Repeat from ★ to continue joining the rows.

Using a crochet hook This is a particularly good method if there is ordinary crochet between the rows of broomstick lace. ★Work two single crochet through both edges of the solid part of the broomstick pattern to join. Pull the loop up until it is the height of the loops in the broomstick pattern to allow it to "disappear." Continue with another two single crochet in the solid sections of the broomstick pattern and join any ordinary crochet rows as usual.

Joining The Starting Chain

These can be crocheted together as usual.

Joining The Curved Tops Of A Broomstick Pattern

The work looks much neater if only the center stitches of each group of loops are sewn or crocheted together, rather than using all the stitches, particularly when taking loops off in groups of four or more. The result is an interesting seam with small open spaces in the shape of diamonds.

Adding Ordinary Crochet

The gauge of a broomstick pattern and that of ordinary crochet using the same hook and the same yarn are quite different. To incorporate crochet into a broomstick pattern it is necessary to compensate for the width of the straight crochet rows. There are two ways of doing this.

Change the hook size This may incur a drop of anything up to four sizes smaller of hook, where there is a noticeable change in the look of the stitch fabric, as the single crochet in the broomstick looks quite slack. With such a hook-size variation, the crochet between the broomstick becomes stiff like cardboard.

Change the number of stitches Use the same hook throughout, but if loops are being removed in groups of five, for example, use only the top four stitches of the group, leaving the stitch lying between the groups unworked. When removing groups in fours, omit one stitch in every two groups and also work the broomstick with one hook size larger than used for the crochet between the broomstick. However, if taking the groups off in three, lose one stitch over two groups, but do not change the size of the hook.

Stitch Library

You can make any number of pleasing designs by simply varying the thickness of the broomstick, the number of loops, and the direction of hook insertion. Try the following examples to see how versatile broomstick crochet is.

Different Thicknesses Of Broomstick

Different effects can be achieved by varying the thickness of broomstick used. Work a length of chain divisible by 4. The test piece begins with 24 chain, using a size 50 (25mm) and also a size 35 (12mm) broomstick.

Row 1: Pick up 24 lps over smaller broomstick, take off in groups of 2 with 2sc in each gr.

Row 2: Pick up 24 lps over larger broomstick, take off in groups of 4 with 4sc in each gr.

Rep rows 1 and 2 to desired length, finishing with row 1.

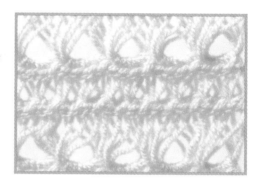

Adding Crochet To Broomstick

Crochet between rows of broomstick needs an adjustment to the number of stitches used in the crochet. Work a length of chain divisible by 5. The trial piece begins with 25 chain.

Row 1: Pick up 25 lps and take off in groups of 5 with 5sc in each gr.

Row 2: Ch2, 1dc in next 8 sts, skip 1 st, 9dc, skip 1 st, 5dc.

Row 3: 1sc in each st to end.

Row 4: ★Pick up 8 lps, pick up 1 lp in the back and 1 lp in the front of the next st, rep from ★ once, pick up 5 lps and take off lps in groups of 5 with 5sc in each gr.

Rep rows 2–4 to desired length.

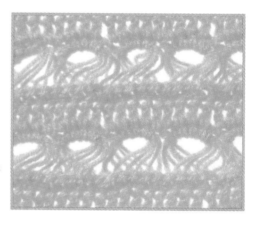

Changing The Look By Changing The Number Of Loops Removed

The fewer loops that are taken off in a group, the longer the drop. Work a length of chain divisible by 6. The trial piece begins with 24 chain.

Row 1: Pick up 24 lps and take off in groups of 6 with 6sc in each gr.

Row 2: Pick up 24 lps and take off in groups of 2 with 2sc in each gr.

Rep rows 1 and 2 to desired length, finishing with row 1.

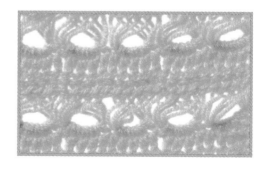

Removing With A Double Crochet

A different look can be achieved by working different stitches.
Work a length of chain divisible by 5. The trial piece begins with
25 chain.
Row 1: Pick up 25 lps, ch2, (this is the starting loop), ★5dc in gr
of 5 lps, rep from ★ to end.
Rep this row to desired length.

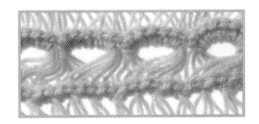

Increasing And Decreasing In Broomstick Lace

Smooth shaping can be obtained by increasing and/or decreasing
over 2 rows. Make a length of chain divisible by 4. The test piece
begins with 24 chain.
Row 1: Pick up 24 lps, take off 1 gr of 4 lps, place 2sc in center,
★4sc in next gr of 4 lps, rep from ★ to last 4 lps, 2sc in last gr
of 4 lps.
Row 2: Pick up 20 lps, take off 1 gr of 6 lps, place 4sc in center,
★4sc in next gr of 4 lps, rep from ★ to last 6 lps, 4sc in last gr of
6 lps (16 sts).
Rep rows 1 and 2 once, losing 4 lps on
each row.
Row 5: Pick up 8 lps, ★place 6sc in gr of 4
lps, rep once.
Row 6: Pick up 12 lps, place 4sc in first gr
of 2 lps, ★4sc in next gr of 4 lps, rep from ★
to end, 4 lps in last 2 lps.
Row 7: Pick up 16 lps, 6sc in gr of 4 lps
★place 4sc in next gr of 4 lps, rep from ★ to
last 4 lps, 6sc in gr of 4 lps.
Rep rows 6 and 7 once.
Fasten off.

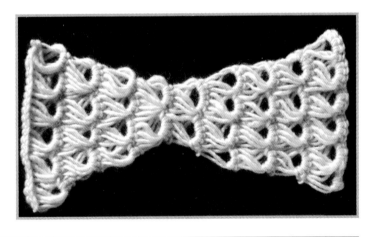

Front-To-Back Hook Insertion

Loops can be taken off to lie in different directions. This looks
effective only if the change is worked in either columns or
rows. Work a length of chain divisible by 5. The trial piece
begins with 25 chain.
Row 1: Pick up 25 lps, 5sc in gr of 5 lps inserting hook in
direction of broomstick tip, ★5sc in gr of 5 lps inserting hook
in direction of broomstick base, 5sc in gr of 5 lps inserting
hook in direction of broomstick tip, rep from ★ to end of row.
Rep this row to desired length.

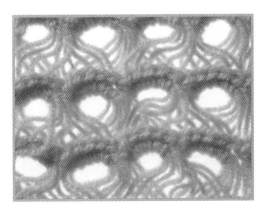

Project 17: Stole

This stylish black mohair stole is worked in two halves and is the perfect opportunity to practice your broomstick technique.

Materials

5 1¾oz. (50g.) balls of Yorkshire Mohair in black (see page 155)
Size 7 (5.00mm) hook
Size 50 (25mm) broomstick needle

Size

Before fringing: 24 x 15½in. (120 x 40 cm.)

Gauge

3½in. (8cm.) over 4 groups (12 sts) and 3 rows to 4in. (10cm.)

First Half

Ch58.
Row 1: Lift 1 lp for each ch onto the broomstick (58 lps). Remove 4 lps, ch1 to beg crochet, 4sc in center of lps, ★ remove 2 lps, 2sc in center of lps, remove 4 lps, 4sc in center of lps, rep from ★ to end (19 groups).
Row 2: Lift 1 lp per st onto broomstick. Remove 4 lps, ch1 to beg crochet, 4sc in center of lps, ★remove 2 lps, 2sc in center of lps, remove 4 lps, 4sc in center of lps, rep from ★ to end.
Rep row 2 16 times. Fasten off.

Second Half

Join yarn to the starting chain with the ridged side of the broomstick pattern at the back.
Work row 1 once and row 2 17 times.
Make a fringe with the remaining yarn by hooking 2 pieces of yarn in each stitch.

CHAPTER TEN

Finishing Workshop

ONE OF THE MOST important aspects of making a crocheted article is how it looks when it is completed. A faultless piece of crochet in the correct yarn and color could prove unsuccessful if it is carelessly finished. Your choice of fastenings, the execution and type of join chosen (when more than one piece of crochet is put together), and, of course, the way it hangs are all important considerations for a professional finish.

Wherever possible, work all crochet in one piece. For example, when working a jacket from a printed pattern it is easy to avoid side seams by working the first front, the back, and the second front as one, separating only at the armholes.

Despite your best efforts, it is possible that heavier pieces of crochet may drop. This is why I suggest crocheting, rather than sewing, seams together, so that they will drop too. If you are making a very long article, such as a curtain, full-length coat, or skirt, pin your crochet to a padded hanger inside a cover, and let it hang between the times you are working on it.

Finishing Your Work

This is the time to personalize your article. Besides executing a professional finish in seams, fastenings, etc., you can include additional features to make it totally individual.

Making Sure The Crochet Pieces Are The Correct Size

1 Before putting any pieces of crochet together, make sure that you have given the crochet a tug in the direction in which is to hang—that is, from top to bottom.

2 All motifs are better joined during making. However, if the article consists of cotton motifs which have not been joined while being made, pin them out to the same size using stainless steel pins. Steam or press with a damp cloth, and leave to thoroughly dry naturally.

If you have worked yarn motifs that have not been joined during making, they should be pinned to size and steamed from about 6in. (15cm.) above the motif, then left to dry before being joined.

Choosing The Right Joining Method

1 Wherever possible join two pieces of flat but solid crochet with single crochet worked on the inside. This is particularly important when joining items worked in yarn rather than thread. The crochet stitch will give in proportion to the rest of the work.

2 A crocheted slip stitch can be used instead of single crochet for a flatter finish. However, slip stitches do not give, so if there is any tendency for the work to drop, the seam will look as though it has been badly put together.

3 If you are sewing a seam, use overcasting rather than backstitch. All sewn stitches are unforgiving and backstitches especially so.

4 Where there is a lace stitch, follow the lace pattern, using the same joining method that you use for motifs. Alternatively, work (2 chains, 1 slip stitch) into second piece, (2 chains, 1 slip stitch) into first piece, to link the two pieces rather than butting them together.

5 Joins for Tunisian and broomstick crochet have been covered on pages 89 and 135. Do refer to these again, as these methods can be helpful for joining other types of crochet.

6 Textured crochet often benefits from having a row of crab stitch worked on the right side of the work to act as a join. The crab stitch then looks part of the textured pattern, giving a lift to the fabric.

Insertion strips can sit flush with the side of the fabric into which they are being placed, or they can overlap the edges for decoration. In the case of an overlap it is advisable to have a decorative edge along both sides of the insertion strip, as you would for a braid (see pages 146–147). However, if the braid is to sit flush with the fabric, the edge of the braid should be straight.

Borders, Edgings, and Ensertions

Ideally borders and edgings should be worked directly onto the article. Even when the insertion, border, or edging is going to be worked separately and then added to an article, try to work a row of single crochet along the edge of the material, whether the fabric is woven, knitted, or crocheted. This gives both stability and uniformity to its appearance and at the same time makes the actual joining much easier.

It is not advisable to work buttonhole bands in a stitch that has a tendency to elasticity. Therefore, where a raised double crochet rib is used for the cuff or waistband, avoid the temptation to working raised doubles for the button and buttonhole bands. Instead use single crochet or slip stitches.

Fastenings

The two most common fastenings are buttons and zippers. Velcro, hooks and eyes, and snaps all tend to tug the crochet unless backed with ribbon. Ribbon is unforgiving and should be used only as a last resort.

Buttons

Bought buttons are absolutely fine to use, and there are some wonderfully fun buttons available, especially for children's articles. However, when you are looking for a button to match the color of the yarn you have just used, you will often be unable to find the right size button in the correct color. Given this, covering buttons is a quick and easy alternative. Just for fun, try the buttons listed in the stitch library on the next page.

In most cases it is not necessary to reinforce the buttonhole, but if you feel that the chain space made as a buttonhole is not substantial enough, overcast around the buttonhole, using the yarn rather than sewing thread. If the yarn is too thick, it is normally possible to split it.

Decorative Clips

Usually available in embossed metal or covered wire, these come in two pieces and hook into each other to look like a brooch. On dense crochet these clips are most effective. The only necessity is to make sure that the fabric is strong enough to support the clips.

Buckles

These can be covered to match any belt that has been crocheted, as an embellishment or as an accessory. Buckles can be with or without a prong or are in two pieces to link into each other.

Zippers

Rather like buttons, zippers are often not available in precisely the right color for the garment just made. Buy the one closest in color and insert it in such a way that the zipper is hidden underneath two edges of crochet.

To make an invisible enclosure, work a row of single crochet followed by a row of crab stitch on the right side of each edge.

Next, on a flat surface, carefully pin the zipper into place, making sure both edges of crab stitch meet and that the crochet is not stretched anywhere.

On the wrong side, using sewing thread, overcast the fabric edges of the zipper to the back of the crochet stitches.

Finally, on the right side, using exactly the same color of thread as the yarn, sew the zipper into position with small unobtrusive backstitches.

Embellishments

A bought article can be embellished using simple flowers, decorative buttons, small motifs, or braids. These can then be appliquéd onto the item in a way pleasing to the eye.

Braids

A braid is different from an edging. An edging has one straight side and one decorative side, whereas both sides of a braid should have an interesting finish, such as scallops, picots, points, etc. Neither side of a braid should be straight, although, as always, there will be exceptions to this rule.

A selection of stitch patterns for braids can be found on pages 146–147.

Choosing Embellishments

When you have completed an item of crochet, I suggest that you put it away temporarily without using it. After two or three days, bring it out for a final assessment. Try not to look at it as you place it at one end of the room. Then, still without looking at it, move as far away as possible. Now observe it with detachment. It will seem different to you because you are looking at the finished item and, hopefully, feeling justly proud.

At this point be critical, in constructive ways, and ask yourself the following questions:

1 Would the addition of a lace motif or flower enhance the item?

2 Would a braid improve and emphasize some of the key lines of the design?

3 Could the addition of one row of single crochet and one row of crab stitch in another color give it a lift?

4 Is there a panel, stripe, or decoration that is distracting the attention and making it difficult to see the item as a whole?

Leave your crochet alone if you answered "No" to all the questions. If you answered "Yes" to questions 1, 2, or 3 add the appropriate embellishment. If the answer to question 4 was "Yes," add a motif or braid to break up the panel
or stripe, or try using a different decoration.

Remember, no two people prefer exactly the same thing, and it is *you* who needs to like the result.

Caring For Crochet

Now that you have finished your crocheted garment, fashion accessory, or home furnishing, you will want to know how to care for it. The following guidelines on washing, dry cleaning, and ironing will help you to keep your crochet looking its best.

Washing

I confess to using the washing machine rather than laundering by hand, but I do take precautions to ensure that the crochet isn't damaged. You may find the following points helpful when deciding how to wash your crochet:

1 Place the crochet inside a pillowcase to avoid unnecessary stretching and knotting.

2 Always choose the temperature according to what is suitable for the fiber content.

3 Cotton articles can withstand a hot wash and full spin. Ideally, you should iron these items while still a little damp and then leave them to lie flat until completely dry. Alternatively, you could pin them onto a sheet and let them dry naturally.

4 Pure wool or mixed fibers respond well to a cold wash. Use a short spin to remove excess moisture, and then allow the article to dry naturally on a flat surface.

5 Mohair will require brushing after it has dried. The type of brush that you would purchase to groom a cat would be ideal for this purpose.

Ironing And Pressing

Ironing and pressing are recommended only with 100 percent cotton crochet. A little spray starch will add a touch of crispness to household linens without discoloring them.

Stitch Library

This library includes patterns for a variety of fastenings. Besides having a practical purpose, all these buttons and braids could be used in art for decorative effects.

Simple "Pierrot" Button

Ch3, join into a ring with sl st.
Rnd 1: Ch3, 1dc in center of ring, join with sl st to top of 3ch.
Rnd 2: Ch1, 1sc in each dc, sl st to join.
Rnd 3: As rnd 2.
Leave a 8in. (20cm.) end of yarn. Using a tapestry needle, weave this end through the stitches. Fill the center of the button very firmly with some of the same yarn. Then use the loose end of yarn to draw the stitches tightly together. Fasten off securely, and use the same thread to attach the button to the article.

Smaller "Pierrot" Button And Variation For Fine And Glitter Yarns

Work exactly as for Simple "Pierrot" Button, but add a fourth round:
Rnd 4: Ch1, ★ sc2tog, 1sc, rep from ★ to end.
This reduces the last round to 8 sts. Complete as for Simple "Pierrot" Button.

Flat Button

Work exactly as the Smaller "Pierrot" Button variation to make a button casing into which you can insert a button mold, bead, or old button. Remember that crochet may stretch, so a tightly fitting button is essential for success.

A Simple "Pierrot" Button made in single crochet.

Two-colored Button

Ch3, join into a ring with sl st.
Rnd 1: Ch1, 5sc into ring with first color. Fasten off.
Rnd 2: With second color ch3, 1dc in same st, 2dc in each sc to end, sl st to join.
Thread an 8in. (20cm.) yarn end through each st and finish as for Simple "Pierrot" Button.

Three-colored Button

With first color ch3, sl st to form a ring.
Rnd 1: Ch3, 8dc in ring, sl st to join, fasten off (9 sts).
Rnd 2: With second color join under 3 (not 2) strands, ★1RdcF, ch1, rep from ★ 8 times, sl st to join. Fasten off.
Rnd 3: In third color join under 3 strands (that is, between the sts), ★bring yarn to front of button, work 1dc in top of dc of rnd 1

Three-colored Button

Simple "Pierrot" Button

A Three-colored Button in a different colorway.

(this is lying free because of the raised dc), 1sc in st, rep from ★ to end, sl st to join. Do not break off yarn (18 sts).

Rnd 4: Ch1, sc2tog, ★1sc, sc2tog, rep from ★ to end (12 sts).

Rnd 5: As rnd 4. Finish as Simple "Pierrot" Button.

Ring Button

Cover any kind of ring (plastic curtain rings are most suitable), with as many sc as possible so that the sts are close together and do not spread. Join with sl st and using a very long thread embroider or weave 8 "spokes" to make an interesting middle.

Buckle

Cover a buckle as you would a ring button with as many sc as possible, making sure the sts are close together and do not spread. Join with sl st. Fasten off.

Two-color Braid
(worked lengthwise)

In first color work enough chain for desired length. Break off yarn. † With rough side of ch facing, join second color to top strand of stitch only, ch1, ★1sc in top lp of next st, rep from ★ to end. Fasten off. Rep from † for other side of chain. Without turning join in first color at left-hand side of work, ch1, crab st to end. Fasten off. Make a second row of crab st along the other edge of the braid.

Three-colored Braid
(worked lengthwise)

In first color work sufficient chain for desired length.

Row 1: With smooth side of ch facing, sc in top lp only along both sides of ch.

Row 2: Do not turn, join second color to beg of row, ch1, 1sc in same place, ★1sc in base of sc for a spike st (i.e. hole in ch), 1sc, rep from ★ to end. Fasten off and rep down other side.

Row 3: Join third color to beg of row, ch1, 1sc in same place ★ch1, skip 1 st, 1sc in sc (i.e. to left of spike and right of sc), rep from ★ to end. Fasten off. Rep down other side.

Flat Button with the addition of crab stitch

Simple "Pierrot' Button

Ring Button

Two-colored Button

Covered Buckle

Two-colored Braid

Vetch Braid

Ch8, join with a sl st to form ring, ch3, 7dc in ring, ch6, sc in ring, turn, ★ch3, 7dc in 6ch sp, ch6, sc in 6ch sp, turn, rep from ★ to desired length.

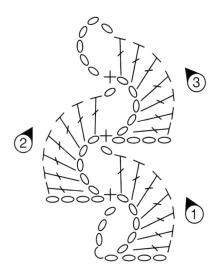

Three-colored Braid

Tailored Braid

Ch4.
Row 1: 1sc in second ch from hook, 1sc in each of 2 rem ch, ch2, turn.
Row 2: 1sc in same place as turning ch, 2sc, ch2, turn. Do not use turning ch.
Row 3: As row 2.
Row 4: 1sc in same place as turning ch, 1tr, 1sc, ch2, turn.
Row 5: As row 2.
Rows 2–5 form patt (see below). Rep patt for desired length. This braid can be applied flat or doubled in half to bind an edge giving a picot look (if necessary substitute a dtr for the tr to give an even more pronounced picot look).

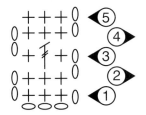

Herringbone Puff Braid

Ch4.
Row 1: (1dc, 1puff st) in 4th ch from hook, ch3, turn.
Row 2: 1puff st bet dc and puff st, 1sc on top of ch, ch3, turn.
Row 3: 1puff st bet dc and puff st, 1sc, ch3, turn.
Rep row 3 to desired length.
2dc in next ch sp, ch5, turn.
Rep rows 2 and 3 to the desired length.

Waterfall Braid

Ch8.
Row 1: 1dc in 5th ch from hook, 3dc, ch5, turn.
Row 2: 1dc, ch1, 3dcl bet next 2dc, ch1, skip 1dc, 1dc, ch5, turn.
Row 3: 2dc in 1ch sp, skip 3dcl, 2dc in next ch sp, ch5, turn.
Rep rows 2 and 3 to the desired length.

Insertion Strip

Ch21.
Row 1: 1dtr in 6th ch from hook, ch5, skip 5ch, 2tr in next ch, 1tr, 2tr in next ch, turn to work over the tr, (ch3, sl st in tr) 3 times, (ch2, 1dc) in tr, turn again, (ch3, sl st in 3ch sp) 3 times, ch3, sl st to tr, ch5, skip 5ch, 2dtr, ch6, turn.
Row 2: 1dtr, (ch4, skip 1 3ch sp, 1dc in next 3ch sp) twice, ch4, 2dtr, ch6, turn.
Row 3: 1dtr, ch5, skip 5ch 1dc, 5tr in next 5ch sp, turn to work over the tr, (ch3, sl st in tr) 3 times, ch2, 1dc in tr, turn again, (ch3, sl st in 3ch sp) 3 times, ch3, sl st to tr, ch5, skip 5ch, 2dtr, ch6, turn.
Rep the last 2 rows to the desired length.

Basic Information

It seems that the versatility of crochet even extends to the words given to describe the techniques. Terms used in crochet do not have a worldwide standard, so the same word can often mean different things in different countries. For this reason, always read the definitions given at the front of any pattern you purchase, to check that you are using the same terminology. The most common variations have been included in the following pages for a quick reference.

Abbreviations

beg	begin(ning)	p	picot
bet	between	patt	pattern
blk	block	quadtr	quadruple triple
C	contrasting color	RtrF	raised triple front
ch	chain	rem	remain(ing)
ch sp	chain space	rep	repeat
cl	cluster	rnd	round
cm.	centimeter	RtrtrF	raised triple triple front
cont	continue	RS	right side
dc	double crochet	Rdc	raised double crochet
dcl	double cluster	RdcB	raised double pushing stem away from front
3dcl	3 unfinished doubles worked in one stitch	RdcF	raised double pushing stem to front
4dcl	4 unfinished doubles worked in one stitch	RdtrF	raised double triple front
5dcl	5 unfinished doubles worked in one stitch	sc	single crochet
		sc2tog	decrease 1sc over 2 sts
		scl	single cluster
dc2tog	decrease 1dc over 2 sts	sl st	slip stitch
dec	decrease	sp(s)	space(s)
DK	double knitting yarn	st(s)	stitch(es)
dtr	double triple	trcl	triple cluster
g.	gram	Tdc	Tunisian double crochet
gr	group	Ttr	Tunisian triple
hdc	half double crochet	tog	together
in.	inch	tr	treble
inc	increase	tr2tog	decrease 1tr over 2sts
incl	includ(e)(ing)	tr3tog	decrease 1tr over 3sts
lp(s)	loop(s)	trtr	triple treble
M	main color	Ts	basic Tunisian stitch
mm.	millimeter	WS	wrong side
		yd.	yard
		yo	yarn over

Symbols

	International symbol	Variations
chain	⦿	●
slip stitch	⌒	●
picot	⬭	⬭
single crochet	+	▮
double crochet	⟊	+
triple	⟊	⟊
double triple	⟊	⟊
triple triple	⟊	⟊
half double crochet	⟙		
raised double front	⟊	⟊
raised double back	⟊	⟊
dc2tog	⋀	⋀
dc3tog	⋔	⋔
inc 1dc	⋁	⋁
popcorn	⬭	
puff stitch	⬭	
basic Tunisian stitch	⟂	
Tunisian cluster	⟂	
Tunisian puff	⟂	
Tunisian decrease	⟂	
Tunisian triple around another stitch	⟂	
broomstick	⟂	

Common Differences In Terminology

United States	United Kingdom
single crochet (sc)	double crochet (dc)
half double crochet (hdc)	half treble (htr)
double crochet (dc)	treble (tr)
slip stitch (sl st)	slip stitch (ss)
triple (tr)	double treble (dtr)
double triple (dtr)	triple treble (trtr)
triple triple or long triple (trtr)	quadruple treble (quadtr)
basic Tunisian stitch	Tunisian simple stitch
gauge	tension
skip	miss

Using British And European Yarns

You will have seen that Rowan yarns—a British brand—have been used for some of the projects in this book; and if you are already a knitter or crocheter you may already be familiar with some other imported European yarns. Although you can often substitute an American yarn for a specified European yarn—provided you get the correct gauge, which usually means changing the needle/hook size—the substitution may not be entirely satisfactory. The reason is that where smooth yarns are concerned, there are few exact matches, and the resulting fabric may be either too stiff or too flimsy. For example, the closest equivalent to a British "double knitting" (DK) yarn may be either a worsted weight (usually thicker) or a sport weight (usually thinner). If at all possible, therefore, it's best to use the original yarn, or a similar European yarn. (See Sources, pages 155–156.)

Left-handed Diagrams

All the techniques and instructions in this book work beautifully whether you hold the hook in your left or your right hand. If you are left-handed, substitute the diagrams given here for those in the main part of the book; or hold those illustrations up to a mirror to see the left-handed technique.

Making A Slip Knot

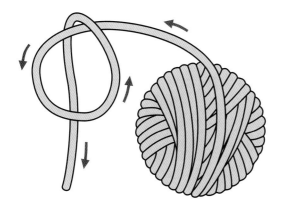

Form a loop of yarn for the slip knot. Insert the hook under the central strand from left to right. (See page 18.)

Holding The Yarn

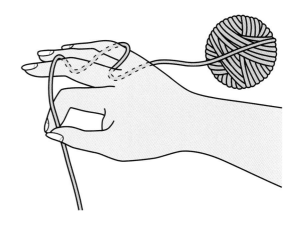

Take the end of the yarn and place it around the fingers as shown. (See page 17.)

Holding The Hook

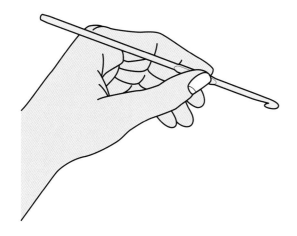

This is one way of holding the hook, holding it as you would hold a pen. (See page 17.)

Making A Chain

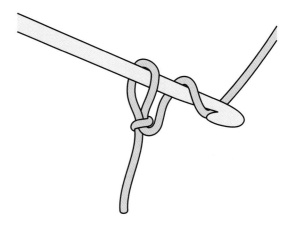

Allow the yarn to come over the top of the hook's stem to nestle in the hook head; draw it through. (See page 18.)

Working A Single Crochet

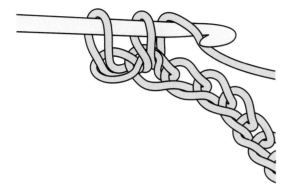

The first single crochet is worked in the second chain. When 2 loops are on the hook, collect the yarn to complete single crochet. (See page 26.)

Inserting The Hook Into Third Chain From Hook

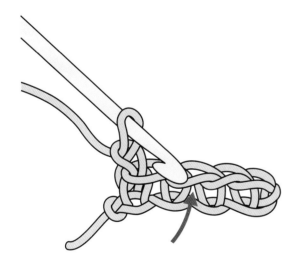

Insert the hook where the arrow points. It is important to remember that the turning chain counts as a stitch. (See page 27.)

Turning Work In Readiness For Second Row

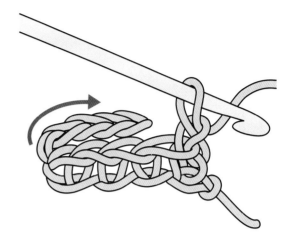

It is easier to find the last stitch of a row if the turning chain is made first and the work turned as shown. (See page 27.)

Commencing A Second Row Of Double Crochet

The loop on the hook does not count as a chain. The hook head shows where the third chain lies. (See page 26.)

Double Crochet

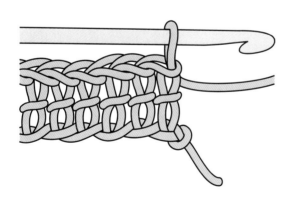

These three illustrations show how to work a double crochet. The double is a longer stitch, in which the yarn is first taken over the hook. (See page 29.)

Crab Stitch

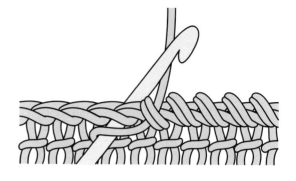

Crab stitch is worked with the front facing and from right to left. (See pages 28 and 29.)

Working The Last Stitch In A Row

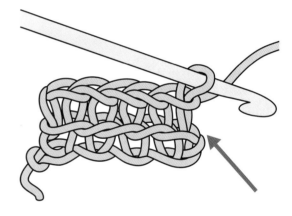

It is easy to miss the last stitch. Check that you have worked the turning chain. (See page 27.)

Working A Decrease

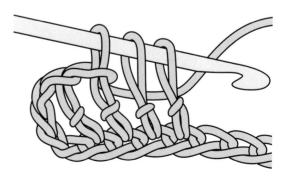

A decrease brings two unfinished stitches together to form one stitch. (See page 55.)

Sources

CMP Habico Limited
Units B4–5
Wellington Road Industrial Estate,
Leeds
LS12 2UA
Tel: 0113 244 9810

Coats & Clark
8 Shelten Drive
Green
SC 29650
Tel: (800) 243 0810

The Craft Collection Limited
Terry Mills
Horbury
West Yorkshire
WF5 9SA
Tel: 01924 810811

Crochet Guild of America
2502 Lowell Road
Gastonia
NC 28054
Tel: (704) 852 9190
(877) 852 9190 (toll-free)

DMC Creative World
Pullman Road
Wigston
Leicestershire
LE18 2DY
Tel: 0116 281 3919

JHB Buttons
1995 South Quince Street
Denver
CO 80231

KCG Trading Limited
PO Box 295,
Huntingdon,
PE29 7HE

Lincatex Limited
Church Cottage,
7 Church Lane,
Stapleton,
Leicestershire,
LE9 8JJ
Tel: 01455 842004

Rowan Yarns
Westminster Fibers, Inc.
5 Northern Boulevard,
Amherst
NH 03031
Tel: (603) 886 5041/5043

Pauline Turner
Crochet Design
Distance Learning Diploma Course
17 Poulton Square
Morecambe
LA4 5PZ
Tel: 01524 831752

Unique Kolours
1428 Oak Lane
Downington
PA 19335
Tel: (610) 280 7720
(800) 25 2DYE4 (toll-free)

Acknowledgments

I wish to thank Coats Crafts UK and Rowan Yarns for the generous use of their yarns. Julia Barnard for selecting the project ideas. Rita, Dorothy, Marie, Marian, Sheila, and all those who crocheted so hard to meet the deadline. The students of the Diploma in Crochet Course who constantly challenge me. Margaret O'Mara for the Tunisian Round Pillow design and Lynne Tuck for the children's Aran Sweater design. A special "Thank you" to Clare Churly, whose eagle eye and constant good humor made writing this book a joy.

Index